TECH TRENDS
OF THE
4TH INDUSTRIAL REVOLUTION

TECH TRENDS
OF THE
4TH INDUSTRIAL REVOLUTION

Dong-Jin Pyo
Jaejin Hwang
Youngjin Yoon

MERCURY LEARNING AND INFORMATION

Dulles, Virginia
Boston, Massachusetts
New Delhi

Publisher: David Pallai
MERCURY LEARNING AND INFORMATION
22841 Quicksilver Drive
Dulles, VA 20166
info@merclearning.com
www.merclearning.com
800-232-0223

D. Pyo, J. Hwang, Y. Yoon. *Tech Trends of the 4th Industrial Revolution.*
ISBN: 978-1-68392-688-7

The publisher recognizes and respects all marks used by companies, manufacturers, and developers as a means to distinguish their products. All brand names and product names mentioned in this book are trademarks or service marks of their respective companies. Any omission or misuse (of any kind) of service marks or trademarks, etc. is not an attempt to infringe on the property of others.

Library of Congress Control Number: 2021934961

212223321 This book is printed on acid-free paper in the United States of America.

Our titles are available for adoption, license, or bulk purchase by institutions, corporations, etc. For additional information, please contact the Customer Service Dept. at 800-232-0223(toll free).

All of our titles are available in digital format at *academiccourseware.com* and other digital vendors. The sole obligation of MERCURY LEARNING AND INFORMATION to the purchaser is to replace the book, based on defective materials or faulty workmanship, but not based on the operation or functionality of the product.

CONTENTS

PREFACE

The term "4th Industrial Revolution" has become commonplace, popping up in various media, but the public's understanding of the underlying technologies is often lagging the fast-pace of its related technological developments. This book is designed to bridge the gap which exists between the 4th industry-related technology boom and the general public's perception of it. The book introduces the content and applications of the related major technologies, such as the Internet of Things, blockchain, artificial intelligence, cloud computing, big data, and robotics – all considered essential for the development and operation of contemporary business models. It is written to minimize technical / engineering content in order to enhance the reader's ability to understand these topics.

Chapter 1 of this book discusses the overall changes in the business environment resulting from the advent of the 4th Industrial Revolution, before going into the details of related technologies. After that, beginning with the introduction of the Internet of Things (IoT), it describes the background, basic concepts, and business applications of the core technologies being used in business operations in the era of the 4th Industrial Revolution. These include cloud computing, artificial intelligence, big data, blockchain, Virtual/Augmented Reality (VR/AR), and robotics.

This configuration is expected to increase readers' understanding of the latest trends – from the concepts of related technologies to their myriad applications. Although the technologies are introduced individually in separate chapters, it should not be overlooked that, in actual business practice, they are organically connected to each other; the IoT plays a role in the process of collecting data off-line, and the storage/processing of massively collected data and big data analysis using artificial intelligence are performed in a cloud computing environment. In addition, blockchain, artificial intelligence, and VR/AR techniques are used in the process to create value by accessing the collected data.

In other words, a series of processes from collecting data to gaining insights for processing, analysis, and decision-making are carried out in an environment in which the aforementioned technologies work organically. These technologies are also used in numerous businesses, such as the financial industry, healthcare, service industries, and in manufacturing, and they are expected to spread in more diverse and converged forms. Therefore, this book is expected to provide useful information to anyone, whether it is a reader with a background in the humanities and social sciences or someone in science and engineering. In addition, it is expected to provide an opportunity for the general consumer, who is living in the era of a paradigm shift, to acquire relevant knowledge within a short time.

Dong-Jin Pyo
Jaejin Hwang
Youngjin Yoon
April 2021

ACKNOWLEDGMENTS

Dongjin Pyo

I would like to thank the publisher and the reviewers. All remaining errors are mine.

Jaejin Hwang

I acknowledge my co-authors, Youngjin and Dong-Jin, who showed the willingness and dedication to complete this book. I would like to thank David Pallai and Jennifer Blaney at MERCURY LEARNING AND INFORMATION, who have contributed greatly toward completing this book. Another acknowledgment goes to my wife, Haewon, for the thorough and insightful comments on the book.

Youngjin Yoon

First, I would like to thank my beloved wife, Bokyung, and my lovely daughters (Ina and Nara). I also acknowledge the publisher and my co-authors, Dong-Jin and Jaejin. Lastly, I want to say that I love my parents and families in S. Korea and the U.K., who have always supported me.

ABOUT THE AUTHORS

Dongjin Pyo (djpyo@changwon.ac.kr) is an assistant professor of the Department of Economics at Changwon National University. He received his B.A. and M.A. degrees in economics from Korea University. He received a Ph.D. degree in economics from Iowa State University. His research and teaching interests include financial economics, agent-based computational economics, and the application of big data analytics to economic analysis. He also has field experience in banking & financial services.

Jaejin Hwang (jhwang3@niu.edu) is an assistant professor of Industrial and Systems Engineering at Northern Illinois University. He received his B.E. and M.S. degrees in industrial and systems engineering from Ajou University. He received a Ph.D. degree in industrial and systems engineering from the Ohio State University. His research and teaching interests include statistical quality control, engineering statistics, reliability engineering, work measurement and design, ergonomics, and occupational biomechanics. He has published more than 50 technical papers, including peer-reviewed journal articles and international conference proceeding papers.

Youngjin Yoon (youngjin.yoon.1220@gmail.com) is the IT Assurance Team Leader at Pitney Bowes and was a consultant at Deloitte with over ten years of broad, global experience (U.S. and Asia). He has experience in diverse consulting projects for over 25 multi-national companies. He received his B.S. in computer science education from Korea University, M.B.A. from Washington University in St. Louis, and M.S in project management from Harrisburg University of Science and Technology. His interests include business strategy & operation, data analytics and visualization, 4th industrial revolution technologies, and risk management.

CHAPTER 1

PLATFORM BUSINESS AS A BUSINESS REVOLUTION

To understand the value of the new technologies (Internet of Things [IoT], cloud, big data, artificial intelligence, blockchain, and virtual/augmented reality [VR/AR]) introduced in this book, we need to understand first the structural change in the overall industrial structure and the new business environment. The structural change of the global economy, also referred to as the 4th Industrial Revolution, can be seen as having an inseparable relationship with the growth of IT technology and related businesses using it.

In the mid-18th century when capitalism was born in the process of the "1st Industrial Revolution," which began in England, technological innovation and new manufacturing processes were introduced into the production process of corporations, and it is fair to say that progress was set to begin around this time. Since then, humankind has made significant progress throughout the "3rd Industrial Revolution," which can be characterized by the invention of internal combustion engines and the growth of the steel, petroleum, and electricity industries, the spread of the personal computer and the Internet, and the rapid development of information and communication technology. These technologies may be taken for granted to the generation who grew up using the Internet and smartphones from birth, but there have been numerous technological and social changes that have evolved over the centuries for them to be created. After a series of industrial revolution processes, we are currently entering the "4th Industrial Revolution" era, which has become one of the most frequently mentioned keywords. Nevertheless, it is hard to define precisely what the 4th Industrial

Revolution means. General definitions of the 4th Industrial Revolution are as follows.

- A fundamental change in the industrial structure that integrates the physical, biological, and digital worlds based on big data and which affects all fields, including the economy and industry.[1]

- An intelligent revolution triggered by artificial intelligence, big data, hyper-interconnectedness, and more.

The previous list does not give a clear answer to our question about the definition of the 4th Industrial Revolution. However, at least the 4th Industrial Revolution's main characteristic is that next-generation industries, which consist of the convergence of the existing industry and information and communication technology, play a crucial role in business and economics. Of course, technology convergence has existed before and has been widely used in business. However, in the 4th industrial era, there is a fundamental change in the way data are created, collected, processed, and analyzed. In other words, in the era before the 4th Industrial Revolution, data only played a secondary role in implementing various business ideas. However, now we are living in an era where new values are created mostly by using data. Furthermore, based on the explosive growth of data, innovation occurs as it is applied to new technologies such as big data analysis, artificial intelligence, cloud computing, IoT, blockchain, and VR/AR. This phenomenon is also related to the emergence and explosive growth of a new business type, namely platform-based business. It is easy to see that there is a sharp contrast between companies that have thoroughly prepared for the 4th Industrial Revolution based on the understanding of its core technologies and those that have not accurately grasped the changing industrial landscape. First, a clear example is Nate-On, a messenger service of SK Telecommunication. Nate-On was a major player dominating the PC-based messenger market in the mid-2000s but missed the opportunity to enter first into the mobile-based messenger service market. The reason for hesitating to develop a mobile-based messenger was worry about the expected decrease in revenue from text-message services. The price for this move turned out to be quite high. In other words, the opportunity to preoccupy the app-based messenger market was taken by KakaoTalk. In particular, in the case of such a messenger service, it is important to create

---

[1] *Schwab, Klaus, 2016, "The Fourth Industrial Revolution," World Economic Forum.*

a network effect[2] leading the market so that users are locked[3] in the service. However, at the time, Nate-On did not preemptively enter the market, despite having established infrastructure and existing users. Therefore, KakaoTalk, which is used by the majority of the Korean people, took over the place, and KakaoTalk's market capitalization currently stands at about 33 billion dollars. Of course, the KakaoTalk messenger service is provided free of charge, but new businesses based on the huge platform that Kakao has built will continue to be developed and expanded. Eventually, it can be expected that the experiment to create new value based on the myriad kinds of data generated by users on the platform that Kakao has built based on messenger will continue.

Another example of failure is LG Electronics' late entry into the smartphone market. Despite the transition to the mobile era when Apple Inc. of the United States launched the iPhone around the world in 2007, LG Electronics was focusing on high-end traditional mobile phones rather than focusing on the development and marketing of smartphones.[4] At that time, LG Electronics possessed the technology and capabilities to transform its core business model to a mobile-based one quickly. However, by not executing a transition to smart mobile devices, its current market share in the global smartphone market is meager compared to other business divisions of LG Electronics. It failed to predict the arrival of the smartphone era when the structural changes in the business environment took place. As a result, LG Electronics' mobile division has been recording losses for 22 consecutive quarters.

Apple Inc., which can be seen as opening the smart mobile era, and Samsung Electronics, a latecomer, are two companies dividing the global smartphone market. Both companies supply their branded smartphones to the global market, but there are key differences between them. First, Apple Inc. does not have a physical production facility that manufactures smartphones, but Samsung Electronics manufactures smartphones directly.

---

[2] *It refers to the effect that the satisfaction gained from using a product or service is determined by how much others use it.*

[3] *It refers to a phenomenon in which, once a consumer uses a product or service, it becomes difficult to transfer demand to other products or services.*

[4] *There is also a rumor that it was McKinsey Consulting, a world-renowned consulting company, who helped adhere to this business strategy at the time. However, LG Electronics denies this, and it is said that McKinsey at the time gave advice on the smartphone operating system.*

Second, the iPhone's operating system is powered by its own iOS and has an AppStore, but Samsung uses Google's Android operating system.

The second difference here is a critical point. In 2008, Apple opened the AppStore, an app store where developers from all over the world can develop their applications and sell them. An important feature of the AppStore is that the development and dissemination of mobile-based app services were made through its operating system and products (e.g., iPhone). Having a popular application platform allows Apple to indirectly hire developers worldwide to provide services without having to create all the apps themselves. It was an attempt to convert the Apple Inc. company to a data-driven platform business firm from a computer manufacturer. Google also developed the Android operating system along a similar path. It can be said that it has opened the stage for developers worldwide to work through Google Play.

As readers can see in the previous example, the most important feature of the 4th Industrial Revolution era is the emergence and growth of platform companies based on data. Based on the spread of smart mobile devices and the app ecosystem, a sharing economy is born, and new financial services and new types of healthcare services are developed. Digital platforms have scalability that can create value in various forms by utilizing the data generated by users to use various services provided on these platforms.

The value of data lies in creating added value by collecting, processing, and analyzing various data derived from the platform business and providing services or goods in areas that existing suppliers could not solve. The growth of this data-driven platform business is also evident in the value of companies currently being evaluated in the stock market. Table 1.1 shows the top ten companies based on market capitalization, with the majority of companies based on online platforms.

Table 1.1. Firm Ranks by Market Capitalization

(As of 9/2/20, Unit: million in USD)

No.	Name	Market Cap	Sector
1	Apple	$2,138,671	IT
2	Saudi Arabian Oil Co.	$1,865,596	Energy
3	Microsoft	$1,733,078	IT

No.	Name	Market Cap	Sector
4	Amazon	$1,704,302	E-commerce
5	Alphabet (Google)	$1,116,804	IT
6	Facebook	$836,931	IT
7	Alibaba Group Holdings Ltd.	$768,931	E-commerce
8	Tencent Holding Ltd.	$666,377	IT
9	Berkshire Hathaway	$524,099	Finance
10	Visa	$459,527	Finance

The growth of platform business based on IT technologies has changed the structure of a market dominated by a small number of participants in the past into a market in which anyone can participate. For example, users can act as both consumers and producers of media content through YouTube. The important feature in such a platform-based business is that the connectivity between different networks or users is a key factor in creating value. In other words, it means that data generated on several online-based networks have become the raw material for creating new business value. Under the conventional business model, the production, distribution, and consumption process of goods and services was in a one-way form. However, now consumers develop services themselves or create data, which has a cyclical structure that feeds back to the supplier. In other words, creating added value through expansion in the direction of creating another value network based on the existing mobile-based network is a vital role of business activity in the era of the 4th Industrial Revolution. From an economic point of view, the 4th Industrial Revolution's core technologies are expected to improve efficiency by reducing transaction costs and information asymmetry within the system.

INTERNET OF THINGS (IoT)

Things and the Internet? Things refer to common objects around us, and the Internet is like a network that connects the virtual world, and at first glance, we cannot find anything in common. However, two words that do not seem to match at all have come together to create a technology called the "Internet of Things," which is already widespread in our lives. So, what is the IoT?

2.1 IoT

The IoT refers to providing new services by connecting objects in the world through wired and wireless networks in various ways. It will be easy to understand that "things" are "connected" to the Internet or a connected network made of things. Unlike the existing Internet, which is connected to through a computer or smartphone that we use, the IoT can be said to be an Internet composed of literally all things[1] in the vicinity connected to a network.

2.2 What Are Things in the IoT?

In the IoT, things are generally known as physical objects (e.g., furniture, automobiles, tools, industrial facilities, manufacturing facilities, industrial robots, products, and electrical equipment around us), and intangible objects (multimedia content and software, spaces such as restaurants, train stations, bus stops, and coffee shops, and business and payment processes) are also included. By connecting various types of objects, the IoT can provide new services that individual objects could not provide. For example, the space in which we live and the objects in our houses (electronics, furniture, lights, etc.) can be connected to each other through the IoT. In

---

[1] *For example, all objects such as cars, bags, cups, beds, and wardrobes can be used.*

addition, living spaces and objects can be connected as one organism to exchange data in real time by analyzing people's movements and patterns through sensors attached to objects (e.g., blinking indoor and outdoor lights and controlling indoor temperature). In this new environment, it is possible to provide a new type of service that enhances our convenience.

2.3 Why the IoT?

According to statistics, as of 2020, the world population was about 7.8 billion.[2] From 2003 to 2020, the population increased by 1.5 billion (from 6.3 billion to 7.8 billion), and equipment that can access the Internet (e.g., computers, smartphones, and wearable devices that could connect to the Internet was 0.08 per capita, and as of 2020, on average, 6.58 devices per capita were connected to the Internet network.

As you might imagine, we could only access the Internet through a computer sitting at a desk until the early and mid-2000s, but after the explosive increase in the spread of smartphones and wearable devices, nowadays we can access the Internet through smartphones, tablet PCs, and wearable equipment (e.g., Apple Watch, Google Glass equipment). Anyone can access the Internet from anywhere and connect various devices. And now, self-controlled machines can perform data collection and transmission without intervention.

In this way, the IoT will change our lives so that people, objects, and spaces that existed separately can be moved to a world where everything is now connected.

2.4 The World That the IoT Is Changing

In this section, we will see how the IoT is changing the world, including some examples.

2.4.1 From Post-Response to Data-Based Proactive Response

The essential part of production facility operation and facility management is maintenance. If maintenance is not performed properly, machines can fail and stop working, leading to a complete factory or facility shutdown. For this reason, the person in charge of maintenance should establish a strategy to prevent risk factors through periodic replacement of parts or safety diagnosis according to the manual. However, each plant operates

---

[2] *https://www.worldometers.info/world-population/*

in a different environment, so the life cycle of the parts will be different. Depending on the circumstance, the life of the machine or parts may be longer or shorter. Even though there are preliminary signs in all accidents, it is not easy to recognize all abnormal signs and respond appropriately to a factory facility consisting of numerous processes and equipment.

What are the advantages if sensors are attached to all equipment in factories and production facilities and then connected to the network? First, data generated from all equipment is collected in real time via the installed sensors, and data analysis can be performed using the collected data. Through this process, monitoring is possible and abnormal signs can be detected in real time. Also, it is possible to predict issues in advance through data analysis rather than post-response. In conclusion, it enables efficient business operation in terms of time and cost and continuous business improvement activities using accumulated data and analysis.

2.4.2 Industry and Business Model Change (from Ownership to Sharing)

The sharing economy is booming all over the world. In the United States, young people in large cities use services such as Uber and Lyft to move rather than buying vehicles and share their homes via Airbnb. You can see many electric scooters for sharing services in urban areas where there is a lot of floating population these days. When traveling and commuting a short distance, you can easily use a scooter after making a reservation/payment through a smartphone app. And when a vehicle is needed, a shared car is rented and used, and IoT technology is a key technology that accelerates this sharing economy.

FIGURE 2.1. Electric scooters (source: "Bird electric scooters in Vienna" by Ivan Radic is licensed under CC BY 2.0).

All information, such as location information of a shared vehicle or electric scooters in motion, a driver's driving pattern, and vehicle status, is collected through built-in sensors. The information is sent to the central management system through the wireless Internet, and it is possible to check the status of the equipment and check the presence or absence of failures through the vehicle's location. The central system can analyze the data for usage of the electric scooter. The data can be used for marketing and promotion by analyzing user movement information, customer usage patterns, and frequency of use by a customer. One of the core technologies that enable this sharing economy business is the IoT.

2.4.3 Innovation in Business Analytics

Most organizations actively use data in decision-making. "Business intelligence" is a tool that helps make business decisions by analyzing existing data based on past and structured data. "Business analytics" is used to provide insights to predict the future through continuous and iterative analysis of data occurring in real time as well as in the past. It goes beyond using general data to find meaning in the data through analysis and to use it for critical decision-making.

Table 2.1 Comparison between Business Intelligence and Data Analytics

	Business Intelligence	Data Analytics
Point of View	Until now (looking backward)	From now on (looking forward)
Question	"What happened?"	"What will happen?"
How?	Dashboard	Prediction
	Tracking	Simulation
	Monitoring	Data Mining
Data Type	Accumulated Data	Real Time Data
	Structured Data	Unstructured Data

For example, if we collected and analyzed data over a certain period generated within the organization or collected externally in the past (sales/accounting/financial/customer-related data, etc.), nowadays, data is collected and analyzed in real time. One of the technologies that made this innovation possible is the IoT.

Geico and Progressive, leading U.S. auto insurance companies, collect raw data using IoT technology to model and analyze an individual driver's risk[3] more precisely. Insurance companies offer their customers premium discounts to allow data to be collected on their driving habits. They send small sensor equipment to customers who are using the car insurance services and have them attach it to their vehicles, install applications on their smartphones, and connect them to the sensor equipment; the companies then encourage customers to use the apps during a certain period for data collection.

The car insurance company calculates individual drivers' risk levels through statistical techniques by analyzing individual driving patterns and habits collected by sensors and transmitted to smartphones, and recalculates insurance premiums based on the risk level. As such, IoT technology provides the basis for providing a service that predicts the future through data analysis and is actively used as a means of business decision-making, such as more sophisticated risk modeling analysis and marketing strategy establishment.

It is also possible to create a market that did not exist in the past by utilizing IoT technology and then making a profit by launching a new business model.

2.5 Characteristics of the IoT and Changes Made by the IoT

Let's look at the IoT's main characteristics and the significant changes caused by the IoT.

2.5.1 Ubiquitous Connectivity

The IoT connects to a network regardless of location through a continuous connection among things and exchanges data interactively. For example, wearable devices like smart watches (Apple Watch or Galaxy Watch) continuously access the network to exchange data in real time, such as movement information, behavior patterns, and users' health information. Self-driving cars would also stay connected by transmitting data in two directions through satellite or high-speed mobile communication networks.

---

[3] *The risks of individual insured persons will differ according to the driver's region of residence, age, vehicle owned, and driving habits. The IoT is used to collect basic raw data for sophisticated statistical analysis.*

FIGURE 2.2. Self-driving car (source: "Google prototype self-driving car" by Marc van der Chijs is licensed under CC BY-ND 2.0).

2.5.2 Widespread Adoption of IP

In order to access the Internet, a device has to have its own address or Internet Protocol. Just as the address given to the home where we live has a unique value without being duplicated, all devices (things) that want to connect to the network have a unique address.[4] This address system is the IP (Internet Protocol). Before the spread of the IoT, PCs or dedicated terminals were used by individuals or companies as equipment to connect to the network. As the number of devices has increased, the number of IP addresses assigned has grown exponentially. Due to the rapid IP spread, the existing IP standard, IPv4, was facing a shortage of addresses; however, this problem can be solved with the IPv6 system[5], which allows more IP addresses.

Table 2.2. Key Comparisons between IPv4 and IPv6

IPv4	IPv6
Deployed 1981	Deployed 1998
32-bit IP address	128-bit IP address
4.3 billion addresses	7.9×10^{28} addresses
Address must be reused	Every device can have a unique address

---

[4] *IP addresses are assigned to objects and unique addresses are used to form a network between objects and to exchange information between objects.*

[5] *IPv4 can create about 4.3 billion Internet addresses (2 to the 32nd power). However, IPv6 can generate 128 squared (4.3 billion × 4.3 billion × 4.3 billion × 4.3 billion) addresses of 2, thus solving the shortage of IP addresses caused by rapid growth of demand.*

2.5.3 Computing Economics

With the spread of the IoT, the amount of data produced has exploded. Also, the generated data is continuously transmitted through the network and accumulated. It is stored in the cloud[6], which is highly scalable and maintained for data collection and storage, and the IoT plays a role in promoting the spread of the cloud. The accumulated data is used as material for big data analysis. This transition makes it easy to collect data that is already widely used for analysis (financial, accounting, sales, etc.) and activities data (location data, behavior patterns, logistics, biology/animal-related research). It accelerates the dissemination of the use of big data analysis. For example, with IoT sensors, personal movement information, lifestyle, health information, and equipment status information in industrial facilities are collected and stored in a cloud database for data analytics in the field. The data collected through the IoT is the basis, and it has evolved naturally into big data as the accumulated scale increases.

Table 2.3. Summary of Characteristics of the IoT and the Changes Made by the IoT

Characteristics of IoT	Changes made by IoT
Ubiquitous Connectivity	The IoT connects to a network regardless of location and type of devices through a continuous connection among things and exchanges data interactively.
Widespread Adoption of IP	As the number of devices is increasing, the number of IP addresses assigned has grown exponentially.
Computing Economics	With the spread of IoT, the amount of data produced has exploded and the accumulated data is used as material for big data analysis.

2.6 IoT Business Application and Use Cases

In this section, we are going to introduce some business applications of Internet of Things (IoT).

2.6.1 Smart Home

In the 1990s and early 2000s, there were many advertisements promoting home appliances based on a future home concept. The ads' main idea was to

---

[6] *Method of using services provided from outside a professional service provider without using the built-in IT infrastructure.*

show an image of a future home, such as making a phone call before returning home, adjusting the house's temperature, cooking on time, and preadjusting household appliances as desired by the user. These advertisements delivered the images of products and brands to customers, and the concept of a so-called smart home has come true thanks to advanced technologies.

A smart home is a technology that connects and controls all devices and appliances in the house, such as TVs, vacuum cleaners, humidifiers, air conditioners, refrigerators, air conditioners, and so forth, and utilities like electricity and water. It refers to a technology that connects energy-related devices such as heating, CCTV, locking devices, and security devices for access control inside and outside the house to the network, remotely controlling and monitoring data.

Smart home users can check the inside of the house with CCTV through a smartphone or other devices from outside or remotely control the operation while connecting the devices with sensors connected to the network and monitoring all related data. All IoT equipment inside the house can be controlled by voice through the artificial intelligence speaker inside the house.

Global home appliance and electronics companies like Samsung and LG have already built a smart home system that can connect their products such as refrigerators, air purifiers, TVs, sound equipment, air conditioners, vacuum cleaners, and intelligent speakers.

Xiaomi is famous for making cost effective products. To use products such as their smart webcams, air purifiers, and smart lights, the company requests users to install an application by Xiaomi to enter its smart home network. It demonstrates that Xiaomi's strategy is not to make profits by selling products but to create its platform and ecosystem. The ultimate goal is to connect its products through a network and accumulate the data collected there. As such, the IoT is used to build such a smart home, and through this, data can be collected/analyzed to provide more customized services to users.

2.6.2 Smart Grid

A smart grid is a combination of "smart" and "grid," which means electricity and gas distribution networks and power grids. It is called the next-generation power grid or an intelligent power grid. The existing power grid has an inefficient structure due to various constraints and limitations in electricity production and distribution. For most goods production is managed according to demand and the supply of products is streamlined through inventory management. In contrast, electricity is a supplier-oriented production where a few producers generate large-scale power generation. When demand exceeds production due to the nature of electricity, for example, if the electricity demand exceeds production due to a heatwave in summer, a large-scale power outage may occur. To prevent it, a power plant produces about 15% more than expected needs.[7] However, if the demand forecast is wrong, the generated electricity cannot be consumed and must be discarded immediately.

The smart grid aims to eliminate such inefficiencies, and the IoT can optimize efficiency by using IT technology. Using a digital meter such as a smart meter equipped with an IoT sensor instead of a conventional meter that measures electricity consumption manually, it is possible to measure and monitor electricity consumption by communicating in both directions with a power company that produces electricity in real time. By comprehensively analyzing real-time data (power usage) collected through the smart meter and various external data (weather, industrial demand, etc.), producers predict the amount of demand close to actual consumption. Also, through this data analysis, producers can analyze energy consumption patterns and trends. This can be used to improve their production systems, revise billing policies, and develop marketing strategies.

From a cost perspective, if IoT technologies like smart meters are used, producers can eliminate manual processes and jobs and energy production efficiency can be achieved, thereby reducing production costs and protecting the environment.

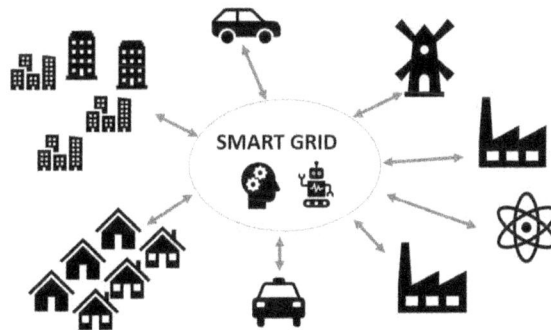

FIGURE 2.3. Smart grid.

---

[7] *It is to produce according to the estimation of maximum power consumption and to secure an extra amount of power in case of an emergency. However, there are inefficiencies for this, such as surplus facilities, use of additional fuel, and disposal of generated electricity, and the use of unnecessary energy adversely affects the environment.*

2.6.3 Smart Healthcare

Smart healthcare is a medical service that combines health-related services with the latest IT technology, providing a comprehensive platform related to medical healthcare. For example, personal health information can be collected through a smartphone or a wearable smart watch, then transmitted to the cloud. A service provider can analyze collected data comprehensively by using existing health examination information, medical records, and drug administration history.

Until now, service providers like hospitals or health insurance companies have led the healthcare service industry. For example, providers of services, that is, doctors, medical institutions, and related companies, were the focus rather than customers or users of medical services. In particular, in terms of information access, the degree of asymmetry between the supplier and the user was severe, and there was inefficiency. The service users faced difficulty in accessing their healthcare information, and it was not properly shared when necessary.

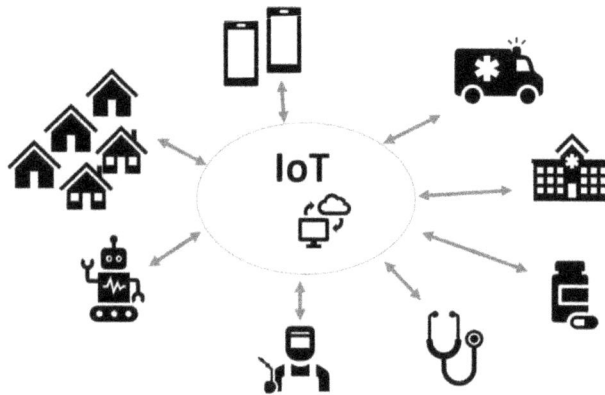

FIGURE 2.4. Smart healthcare.

It was not easy to share information among medical institutions for various reasons (e.g., regulations, customs). So, it could add value by utilizing data compared to other areas. With the application of the IoT, it is possible to collect and share health information such as personal behavior patterns, dietary habits, heart rate, blood sugar, and blood pressure in real time. Based on past medical history and health history information, technology can predict and prevent individual health issues that can change the healthcare direction and approach.

In addition, users of medical services can actively participate in improving service quality themselves. Based on the data provided by the patient, the service provider can customize/personalize medicine that reflects the differences and characteristics of each patient, and the patient will actively contribute to the evolution of a new type of medicine (e.g., participatory medicine).

This paradigm shift can be implemented through data collection through the IoT and technologies such as the cloud and big data. In particular, IoT technology will play a key role in collecting, transmitting, and analyzing data, which is the raw data necessary for analysis.

2.6.4 Smart Shopping

The IoT can change the traditional shopping model in terms of consumer experience and supplier operations. The distributor and retailers can check the location of products and inventory quantity in real time through IoT sensors. It is possible to increase inventory management accuracy through location warehousing and delivery tracking, thereby increasing efficiency in management and operation. From the point of view of store operation, retailers can recognize customers who visit the store to purchase goods with a sensor at the entrance and see whether they are loyal customers with high profitability or not. Then they can be classified and identified in advance through the past purchase history and purchase amount.

Customized promotions or responses are possible through the classification of customers identified in real time and purchase propensity. Previously, retailers conducted surveys to obtain customer feedback by spending money to determine customer satisfaction. In the smart store, customer movement, activity patterns, and patterns of staying in a specific area are tracked using sensor cameras, which are collected and analyzed. The result of this analysis is transmitted to store employees in real time. If necessary, it will promote purchases by providing customer service or sending information such as promotions to the customer's smartphone. It will also be possible to provide a high-level shopping experience to customers by collecting the number of store visitors, demand, and so on, by real-time monitoring and analyzing it to adjust the store environment, such as through store layout reorganization and product rearrangement, to the changing tastes of customers.

As the IoT is applied to the shopping environment, customers can receive customized services. For example, when an individual customer enters a store, the system recognizes the customer through a sensor and combines customer preference information such as tags, style, and color of the customer's clothes, current temperature, recent weather, and fashion information. It is possible to induce purchase by continuously exposing information such as customized recommended products and promotion events on a display screen located on their move. When paying for a product, customers can use the credit card information registered in advance or the credit card chip to line up and leave the store without paying at the clerk.

An unmanned store is possible by making automatic payment through a scanner located at the entrance. Also, customers can accurately grasp product inventory information being aggregated in real time in advance and accurately determine with their smartphones whether a product is located in a store.

Amazon Go, the first offline store launched by Amazon, a global e-commerce market, is a prime example. Amazon Go aims to become a completely unmanned store with a system in which there are no employees in the store and all products are automatically paid for when customers visit, select products, and leave the store. Advanced technologies such as artificial intelligence, machine learning, computer vision, and big data analysis are being applied, among which IoT is the core technology. Consumers download the app on their smartphone, enter the store and select a product, and then leave. It will be paid for via the connected credit card.

FIGURE 2.5. Amazon Go (Source: "Amazon Go at Madison Centre" by SounderBruce is licensed under CC BY-SA 2.0).

2.7 The IoT and Technology Convergence and Value Creation

The IoT itself is meaningful, but it is a technology that can maximize its value when it is combined with other technologies. The core of the IoT is collecting data produced by objects through sensors attached to things. Therefore, it is necessary to store and manage the data collected through the IoT effectively, and the purpose of the IoT can be achieved by analyzing data to create value. To maximize the value of data collected through the IoT, cloud technology is needed for data storage and big data[8] technology for analysis.

Data produced by numerous equipment and devices must be easily and efficiently stored. But the amount of data has increased to a level that is difficult to handle directly within individual organizations. Data is already accumulated through attached sensors not only from electronic devices used by individuals, home appliances, and objects such as automobiles, but also from offices or stores that sell products. "Value" is created in the process of analyzing and storing such data in real time and using it for individuals or industrial sites through analysis and reprocessing. In the whole cycle of this value-added production process, the IoT, cloud, and big data technologies can be combined and utilized as one technology. The data collected through the IoT can be provided as material necessary for learning artificial intelligence. It has the possibility of fusion with other technologies such as blockchain, VR/AR, and robotics automation.

The data that can be collected and stored through the technology of the IoT increases indefinitely, but focusing only on collecting data through the sensor of the device or focusing only on the connection between things is not the core value that can be obtained through the IoT. How to use the data collected through this is the key, and the ultimate core value that the IoT technology can give us is the ability to provide new value to users by processing the insights or data obtained through the data. It is necessary to understand what people want, collect, find new business opportunities from the accumulated data, and discover suitable models. For example, after establishing a smart home, a vast amount of data can be collected through the IoT. It is possible to develop and provide a new service model called personalized service by analyzing the collected data and by identifying customer behavior patterns and requirements. Also, personal health

---

[8] *It refers to a series of processes from the beginning of data to the end of use such as data collection, processing, storage, and analysis.*

information, movement information, and eating habit information collected by IoT sensors in the healthcare field can be analyzed and processed using artificial intelligence or machine learning technology to provide personalized health assistant services. We can achieve the ultimate benefit from the IoT in the smart home/healthcare through this process.

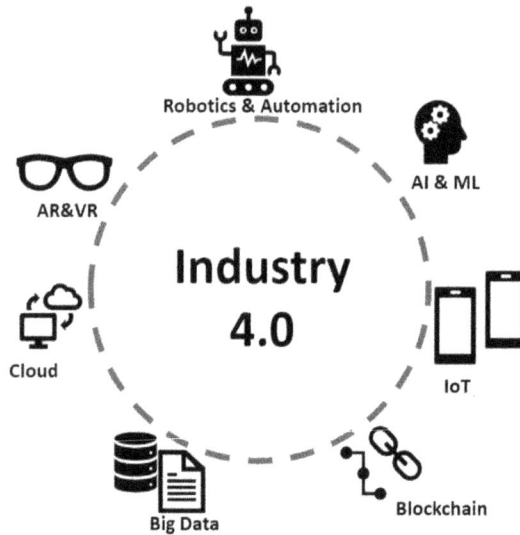

FIGURE 2.6. Industry 4.0 core technologies.

2.8 IoT Market Outlook

According to IDC (International Data Corporation), a specialized market research organization, IoT-related investments and expenditures are expected to grow by more than double digits in 2021 globally, and an annual growth rate of 11.3% from 2020 to 2024.[9] The spread of the IoT is expected to accelerate further due to the global pandemic caused by Covid 19. It has become clearer why companies should develop strategies and road maps to respond to crises through technologies such as the IoT. In 2019 alone, about 1.3 billion devices (things) were connected to the network, which is expected to increase further in the future. As these numbers indicate, if things around us are connected at this rate and grow at this rate, we will easily feel how the IoT affects our lives and why it is important to us.

---

[9] *https://www.idc.com/*

CHAPTER 3

CLOUD COMPUTING

3.1 Cloud?

When purchasing a computer, the hard disk's capacity was an important factor in terms of purchase. Now we take photos and videos anytime and anywhere with a smartphone and watch videos on YouTube regardless of time and place. Physical storage space like a hard disk is much less critical than in the past, since data can be uploaded to the cloud space provided by many online service companies (e.g., Google or Dropbox) and downloaded anytime, anywhere. If you take a photo or video on your smartphone, you can upload your photo to the cloud storage space through the Google Photos app and save it permanently without any restrictions.

Users can check uploaded files through various devices. When collaborating with friends and coworkers in the past, we had to go through the process of delivering the documents via email or USB and collecting the documents separately. But now, multiple users can work on a document simultaneously via Google Docs or MS OneDrive, a service based on a technology called the cloud.

In the past, when we purchased a computer, we had to buy and install software like MS Office first. Purchasing software at a lump sum was economically burdensome in some ways, and the process of upgrading the software version was also inconvenient for users.

These days, there is no need for a company or an individual to purchase and install the software directly. We can instead borrow only as much as necessary and pay a monthly fee for use. Suppose the system is borrowed and used in the SaaS (Software as a Service) method, a cloud form. In that case, users only need to access the software online and use it as much as necessary. The cloud software company will resolve things such as errors, maintenance, and version upgrades.

This is the change in our lives that occurred with the introduction of the cloud. The cloud is a technology that is the foundation for our society to be digitalized. It contributes significantly to accelerating our society's transformation into the 4th industry through convergence with other technologies such as big data, the IoT, and artificial intelligence. Let's take a closer look.

3.2 What Is the Cloud?

The cloud is the immediate provision of system resources and IT resources of virtualized computers. It is a type of network-based computing, which refers to a technology that processes information with other computers connected to the cloud (Internet) rather than one's own computer. Various components, such as CPU, memory, and hard disk, are gathered to create computing power in a computer, and owners use computing resources for their purposes. But when they use the cloud service, they are not using the resources of the computer they are currently using, but instead are using the virtual computing resources on the cloud. As an extreme example[1], an individual can connect to the Internet with a laptop with only a screen and a keyboard and use software in the cloud to do everything, such as playing games, working on documents, and watching videos.

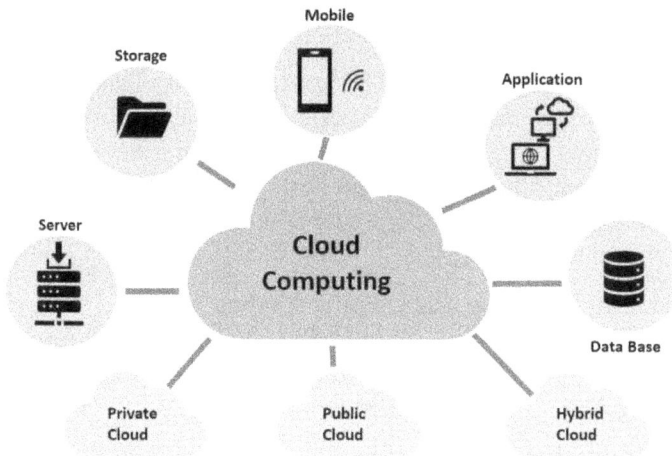

FIGURE 3.1. Cloud computing.

---

[1] *Google Chromebook is an example. Chromebooks do not install and use software on their own, but connect to a network and use software in the cloud. So the price is relatively cheap compared to other laptops.*

In a cloud environment, individuals do not own the necessary computer resources, such as hardware and software, which are the essential elements required to use a computer, but rather borrow and use as much as they need. In the case of companies, the server, database, and necessary enterprise software could be purchased and owned directly, but in the cloud environment, they are not directly purchased, maintained, and managed, but are borrowed and used only as needed, and the usage fee paid. It is easy to understand if you think of it as a direct purchase and ownership method before the cloud era, while the cloud is a rental method.

How is the cloud more advantageous than buying and owning directly, and is the trend of usage changing? It is necessary to understand how organizations operate and manage their IT infrastructure and how IT investments are being made.

3.3 Traditional Infrastructure Model

Organizations and companies of a certain size or larger operate their own IT departments or IT-related support departments. The IT support function is key to corporate sales activities and support. There are two simple activities in the IT department: the first is to introduce/implement a new system and the second is to manage (maintain) the existing system well. Let's look at the traditional IT investment model through a hypothetical scenario on how IT business operates within an organization or company.

Suppose a large retail company named A introduces a new enterprise resource planning (ERP) system or sales management system. Organizations with tens of thousands of employees and tens of billions of dollars in daily sales will perform large-scale IT projects that require at least millions of dollars to deploy such a system. Let's look at the details of the cost components incurred when introducing a new system.

1. Hardware equipment (server/database/network equipment, etc.)

2. Software purchase (ERP or sales management software/operating system/database software)

3. Consultant, developers, maintenance personnel for system implementation

When introducing the system, there is no need to purchase the highest specification product. Based on analysis of the company's size and expected transactions, the system can be developed by considering the appropriate capacity (a level that can handle the maximum usage). Let's assume that the system was developed at tremendous cost through capacity calculation, and after a few years, the company's size (sales, # of employees, etc.) grew and the volume of transactions increased, and the system crashed due to high volume of transactions. So, considering the peak season usage, a new IT investment had to be decided, and with this investment, servers and databases were expanded, software was upgraded, and network equipment was expanded.

Companies must make choices that maximize the effectiveness of their investment. Was this investment the best option the company could make?

3.4 What about Reality?

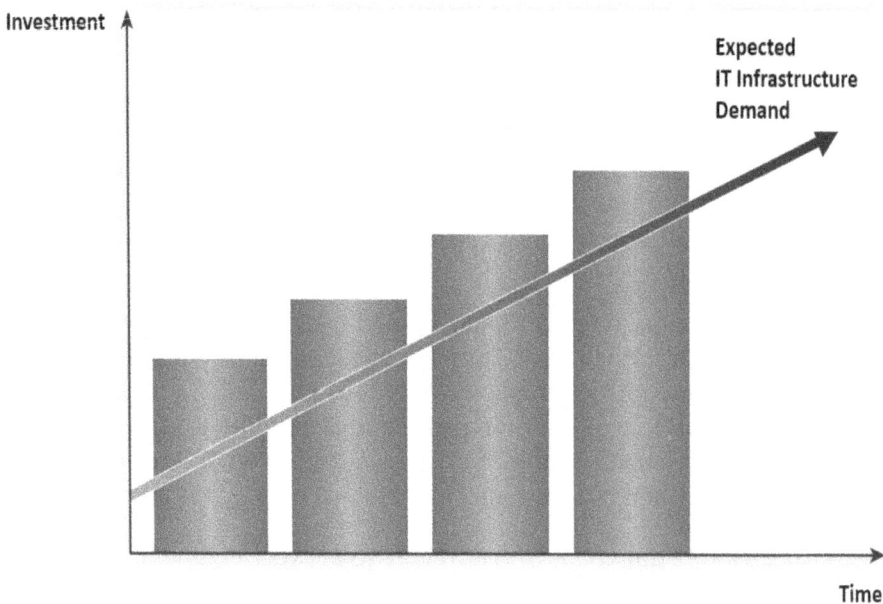

FIGURE 3.2. System processing capacity introduced through IT investment.

Let's take a closer look at what happens in a hypothetical scenario. The previous bar graph is the system processing capacity[2] introduced due to IT investment. The X-axis is the cost investment, the Y-axis is the time, and the line graph is the expected IT infrastructure demand. For example, let's say that a company that operates an online shopping mall does not expand servers in preparation for the explosive increase in visitors during the holiday season and the system is down. Since this is a critical situation for online shopping mall business operation, the company must always have a processing capacity that exceeds the expected maximum required value. However, the reality is that, except for the holiday season, a surplus[3] of computing resources occurs.

It is the same for individuals. For example, when purchasing a laptop, we bought an expensive PC capable of playing high-end video games. But in some cases, we are using the expensive PC only for writing documents or surfing the Internet. It is not an act of rational consumption or investment because the usefulness is low based on the cost-benefit analysis. Conversely, if you want to buy an inexpensive, low-end laptop and want to play a high-end game, this is also an investment failure because it hasn't achieved the desired purpose.

In the business world, in preparation for the worst case, we have to invest in IT, which always leads to excess IT resources. Therefore, it cannot be said that this surplus capacity is necessarily bad, because it is difficult to accurately predict the demand generated in the real world, and its volatility and uncertainty are large. From the standpoint of a company, it is crucial to maximize the effect through investment, but it is not an easy investment decision, because the surplus capacity and shortage occur alternately.

---

[2] *The number of transactions that can be processed or the capacity to process business performance.*

[3] *There may be situations in which the computer resources held for only one month of the year are used to the maximum, and less than half of the remaining 11 months are not used.*

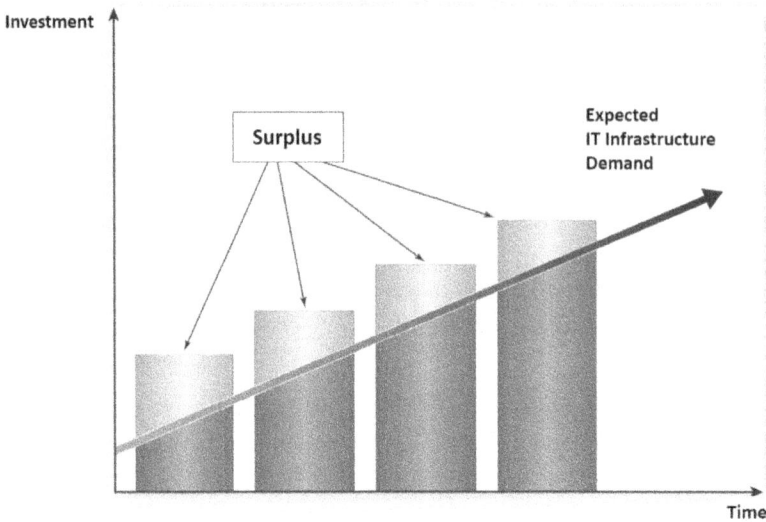

FIGURE 3.3. When IT infrastructure demand is predictable: For business continuity, an investment beyond demand must be made, resulting in a partial surplus of resources. It leads to a certain amount of wasted cost and opportunity cost.

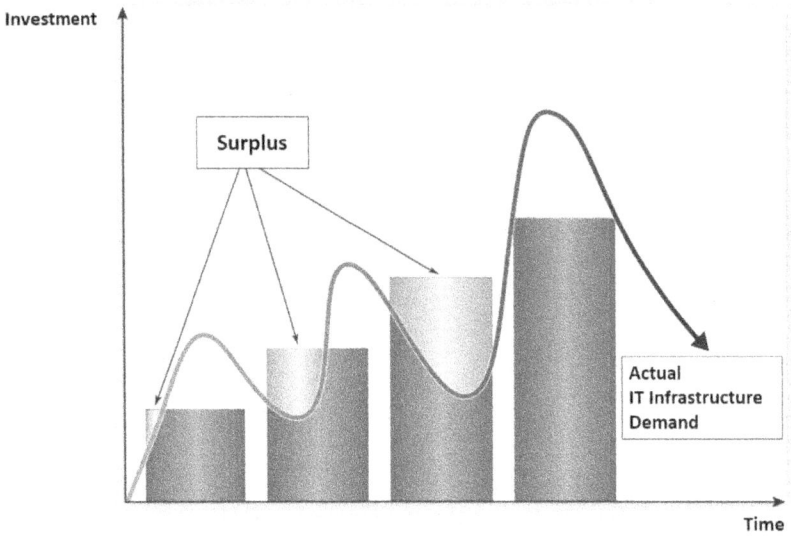

FIGURE 3.4. In the case of irregular fluctuations in demand for IT infrastructure in a real business environment: Due to the high volatility of demand, it is highly likely that the surplus and shortage of resources alternate. Efficient operation is difficult.

3.5 Is It Better to Borrow Than to Own?

From now on, let's look at a new IT investment and operation model through the Utility Infrastructure Model Concept.

3.5.1 Utility Infrastructure Model Concept

A utility refers to the electricity, water, and gas that we use. Consumers use resources and services like electricity and gas through specialized companies rather than owning and operating power generation facilities directly. And you pay only for what you use. Using an IT system through a utility infrastructure model, in other words, means that the user does not own the computer hardware or software, but instead borrows and pays for the use of the hardware or software of a computer owned by professional service providers.

Cloud services are being implemented based on this model, and cloud service providers generally have a reasonable and detailed pricing structure and billing system, so users only have to pay for what they use. Therefore, if an online shopping mall uses the cloud for its operation, it is unnecessary to directly purchase servers and databases that are not needed during the year's downtime due to its seasonality (the explosive increase of visitors only for one month a year). They can pay only for what they use.

Also, the cloud service is operated by professionals who can provide high-quality services. They will provide services in infrastructure areas, such as servers, databases, and networks, and in all areas of IT support, such as customer service centers and cybersecurity.

3.6 What Are the Advantages of Using the Cloud?

First, there is an effect of cost reduction. Instead of investing huge capital in IT facilities, it is often far more advantageous to pay monthly bills for what you use. In particular, when initial investment costs are burdensome, like with small start-ups, this monthly plan is much more attractive.

Second, it is possible to prevent surplus resources due to excessive investment, and it is possible to flexibly respond to unexpected additional IT resource needs (when IT resource usage explodes). As shown in Figure 3.4, it is practically impossible to predict the usage of IT resources accurately.

Only when investing in consideration of the maximum value can risks with large uncertainties (e.g., financial or operational losses due to idle resources and exploding demands) be reduced through the cloud.

Third, cloud services allow users to focus on their core business by entrusting IT services to experts. It is like outsourcing some internal IT management tasks. Therefore, users can pay attention to the service quality. For example, when operating an online shopping mall, the shopping mall operator only needs to concentrate on the business itself when using the cloud. For parts related to IT infrastructure, the management can get professional services from cloud service providers. Instead, it only has to pay attention to the service's quality, continuity, and the cost (bills!).

3.7 Cloud Service Model Type

So far, we have looked at the overall background of the cloud concept. Then, when you decide to adopt the cloud, you need to think about what to do and how. Cloud services are also classified according to type (SaaS, IaaS, PaaS) and deployment (public, private, hybrid) types. Let's find out about those types.

3.7.1 SaaS – Software as a Service

SaaS refers to software operating in a cloud environment, that is, cloud application services. Users do not need to install software on their local PC but connect to the Internet and then use the software via the cloud. Unlike in the past, where necessary software was installed and used on one's own computer, all services are provided in the cloud under the SaaS environment, and the software can be used by accessing the Internet without any installation process. In the past, software had to be purchased, and users owned the license and installed it on their computer and used the software. But in a cloud environment, they only borrow and use as much as necessary. For example, when using an email service, rather than installing Outlook on your computer and using email, in the case of a webmail service, users can use webmail services such as Google, Yahoo, and Hotmail without installing software when sending and receiving emails. You can think of this as an example of a cloud in the form of SaaS.

In the same way, representative ERP systems such as SAP, Oracle ERP, and so on were built-in and operated in the past, but the versions released recently can be used in the form of cloud SaaS that can be accessed and used through the network. The characteristic of SaaS is that users can use the service immediately by signing up when needed and paying for what they use. In the past, users had to install software on infrastructure (server, database) to build the system, but this process is unnecessary now. It has the benefits of reducing time and cost, and a cloud SaaS service provider handles maintenance, so users do not have to worry about version upgrades or patching. Most of the recent software is being released in the cloud, and representative example products and services are as follows:

- Most of Google's products
- MS Office 365
- SalesForce.com (CRM)
- SAP HANA
- Oracle ERP

In the case of the Google Chrome laptop on the market, all software, including the OS, is designed to be used in the cloud, so the hardware is customized based on this environment with a minimum specification to run cloud-based software, so users can purchase it at a relatively low price.

3.7.2 PaaS – Platform as a Service

Platform as a service (PaaS) is a service that supports the various support systems (platforms) necessary for software developers who develop applications in the cloud. When developing systems or applications, multiple infrastructures such as development, testing, and operating environments are required. PaaS allows users to focus on development itself in a virtual environment provided by a cloud service provider without the need to build and maintain it by users. For example, a cloud service in the form of SaaS is like a form that provides customers with delivered food and the customer simply enjoys it, whereas PaaS is like a type of meal kit which is ready to cook with no need for prep. PaaS can provide all of the various complex cooking tools or equipment to cook (software). In the case of PaaS, cloud service providers give the developers an environment to create, host, and deploy applications. Therefore, PaaS allows developers or their teams to focus entirely on application development, improving a product's quality.

3.7.3 IaaS – Infrastructure as a Service

In IT, infrastructure usually refers to physical equipment. For example, many machines, such as servers, storage, and network-related equipment, are stored and operated in a data center. In the past, companies managed to run IT teams or computer rooms directly. In small organizations, a server room is operated in one room of the building, and several servers are placed there. Any organization that operates such physical spaces and equipment requires a budget for operation facilities and employees, but managing infrastructure in the cloud is not what we own. It borrows infrastructure resources for servers and storage in data centers operated by specialized cloud service providers. Users do not need to purchase equipment that needs to be expanded or newly implemented as needed, and they only need to borrow and use infrastructure resources operated by service providers in a cloud environment without hiring personnel.

In the infrastructure (server, database, network) used in this way, users can install any software as desired and use IT services if necessary. In addition to the cost aspect, it is good to use the infrastructure in the form of the cloud to receive specialized services for infrastructure operation. In many cases, a business operation continuity[4] problem occurs due to infrastructure operation failure. In this case, it is advantageous to use a specialized company's services rather than internally performing backup and recovery.

For these reasons, many online service companies use IaaS services, and Netflix is a prime example. Netflix is a global online streaming service company that provides movies and dramas with tens of millions of people connecting simultaneously. Video services are provided through real-time streaming, which might cause massive damage to the company's brand or reputation if the service is temporarily unavailable due to a huge amount of traffic and data usage. Also, the industry has a large seasonality during peak season, where the number of visitors explodes during specific periods such as weekends and the holiday season. For this reason, Netflix closed its own data center and moved all infrastructure to AWS (Amazon Web Service), a leading cloud company, and is using infrastructure services flexibly according to demand. For example, when the number of users is low, the infrastructure used can be reduced easily, and when the number of users is increased during peak times, the number of servers required is increased with just a few clicks to respond to exploding demand flexibly.

---

[4] *If the system is down due to server problems, hacker attacks, or natural disasters, business shutdown and customer churn can seriously affect sales and profits.*

Table 3.1. Cloud Service Model Type

Cloud service model type	Examples	User
SaaS: Software as a Service	Google Docs, SalesForce	End customers
PaaS: Platform as a Service	App Engine, Azure	Developers
IaaS: Infrastructure as a Service	Amazon Web Service	System admins

3.8 Cloud Service Model by Type of Deployment

There are three types of cloud service based on their deployment model. We will see the three types in this section.

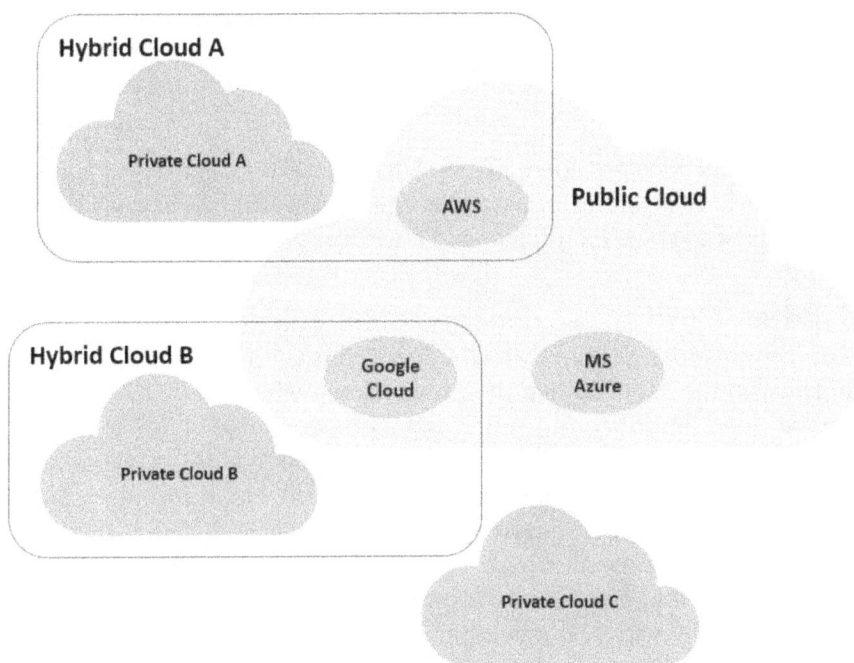

FIGURE 3.5. Cloud service model example.

3.8.1 Public Cloud

The public cloud model refers to a cloud environment that can be accessed and used by anyone who would like to use the service. Computing resources such as servers or storage are owned/operated by external cloud service providers, and anyone can access and use them through the Internet. In other words, anyone who is willing to pay for the service can subscribe to and use services such as Amazon Web Services (AWS) and MS Azure, which are widely used. When using the public cloud, users feel as if they are using independent services in a virtualized form, but in reality, they share the same server, storage, and network equipment physically with other organizations or users.

In addition to cost reduction and maintenance convenience, the advantages of the public cloud are the following:

- **Scalability**

  Computer resources can be changed quickly and flexibly by increasing and decreasing IT services' usage on demand to meet all business operation requirements such as an unexpected increase or decrease in use.

- **High stability**

  Cloud service providers already have vast server capacity, business processes, and experts prepared for emergencies and disasters. Therefore, users can receive professional IT services based on high stability.

3.8.2 Private Cloud

The private cloud is literally a cloud environment in which use is allowed only to limited users, unlike the public cloud, which anyone can use. The public cloud described previously is a method in which a service provider owns system resources and lends them to users. In a private cloud, a user or an enterprise directly develops and owns the cloud system resources. The user or enterprise builds and uses its dedicated cloud. In the case of large global corporations, if they build a private cloud at the global headquarters and give access to branch or office employees worldwide and use it only within the company, this is a private cloud. The private cloud is not operated by an external service company but is maintained and managed within the organization, so all equipment and software are used exclusively. There is a lot of room to adjust and change to fit. Also, because the cloud resources and stored data are in the organization, owners have control over IT resources, and they can maintain high security by storing the data inside their network. Because of this, the government, financial institutions, or organizations dealing with sensitive information prefer the private cloud.

3.8.3 Hybrid Cloud

As the name suggests, the hybrid cloud is a method of mixing public and private cloud environments. The environment is configured so that the cloud environment is located inside the organization, and a part of the public cloud is used simultaneously for external computing resources. For example, the private cloud can be used for IT resource backup, disaster recovery, test/development, and so on, and the public cloud can be used for other purposes (using the SaaS software).

Table 3.2. Cloud Service Model Type

Cloud service model by type of deployment	Summary
Public Cloud	Provisioned for public users and open to anyone who needs cloud service
Private Cloud	Used for a single organization
Hybrid Cloud	Composition of two or more clouds (public and private)

3.9 Introducing the Cloud Business Case

Cloud adoption has the advantage of preparing for traffic congestion and strengthening IT security. Let's look at a real case of adopting a real cloud.

3.9.1 Healthcare

The cloud can be actively applied in the healthcare field. It can be used to respond flexibly to the gap between supply and demand in the healthcare market. Demand for healthcare is expanding with the aging population and the improvement of a healthy life span. For example, with the development of medical devices and healthcare digitization, patient data has increased countlessly. Cloud infrastructure makes it possible to efficiently store and process such a wide range of healthcare information. Microsoft released a preview of the "healthcare cloud"[5] for the healthcare industry. Microsoft Healthcare Cloud enables medical institutions to deliver management plans and preventive support for individual patients on any device (computer, smartphone, tablet, etc.). Also, the opinions of medical staff can be shared, which makes it easier to analyze and manage the views, including patient satisfaction.

---

[5] *It is a medical SaaS solution and can be integrated with the existing electronic health record and platform. Users can access and use the cloud.*

3.9.2 Agriculture

In the field of agriculture, innovative examples of cloud adoption are also being created. Using the cloud platform makes it easy to collect and manage data of various types of equipment in a standardized manner. It allows more flexible follow-up management, as it may not be limited to the use of existing products. Furthermore, it becomes possible to manage a broader range of root growth monitoring and control beyond the existing temperature and humidity control by using cloud services. The big data accumulated in the cloud can be analyzed and utilized, and it is expected to be of great help in scientific farming. Also, Alibaba Cloud Company manages the pig farming business by applying its new cloud technology based on Alibaba Cloud's self-developed Artificial Intelligence (Project Title 'ET Agricultural Brain'). By monitoring visual and audio data and changes in the real-time environment, each pig's activity patterns, growth indicators, pregnancy, and other health conditions will be managed. It has created an effect of increasing the production of pig farms and reducing abnormal piglets' mortality. Such cloud-based smart farm management is expanding to various agricultural fields, including fruit tree cultivation operations.

3.9.3 Entertainment

The game industry is the most significant area of cloud applications. Cloud games are a way to play games by streaming them to the screen of other devices without a gaming PC through a high-performance server. High-speed networks are essential for such cloud games, and performance is improving due to the advent of high-speed networks such as 5G and Wi-Fi 6. Running Xbox games in Microsoft's data center supports an environment where we can enjoy a much faster and more vibrant game. As a result, it is possible to enjoy seamless online action games and fighting games. Also, Sony PlayStation provides a cloud streaming game service called "Now." In total, it offers more than 750 streaming games for the PlayStation 2, 3, and 4. These cloud streaming games are expected to continue to evolve with the evolution of the network.

3.10 Introduction of Representative Cloud Services

Now let's look at representative cloud services. Amazon Web Services (AWS) is a cloud computing platform developed by Amazon. AWS was established in 2006 and provides IaaS that rents infrastructure, such as a large number of servers and storage spaces, to users. It is known as the number one cloud service market share globally, and numerous customers such as Netflix and NASA are its clients. At the beginning of their business, Amazon felt the need for cloud computing for its core business, the online e-commerce business, and launched AWS to solve their problems. Now AWS is generating higher revenue than its traditional business model (e-commerce sector).[6] Amazon uses EC2 (Elastic Compute Cloud) to acquire new servers, shorten boot time, and quickly adjust computing power according to computing requirements. With this resizable computing power, users pay only for the amount they use. Networking services allow users to directly control the virtual network environment, allowing them to use the environment as if they were in an existing network. And they offer a variety of storage options depending on the type of data and usage. One of the reasons AWS has attracted many customers is its low cost. It operates on a pay-as-you-go system where users pay only for what they use, without prior confirmation or long-term commitment. There is no need to pay for data center operation and maintenance. And in minutes, the platform can be deployed globally, showing great agility. Thus, it has a wide range of users, including enterprise, start-up, and public sector customers.

Microsoft Azure is a public cloud platform provided by Microsoft. The Azure platform integrates two services: IaaS with infrastructure structures such as servers, storage, and networks, and PaaS, which provides an application development environment. Microsoft Azure features have high compatibility[7] with existing Microsoft products, and it is possible to switch from the system environment in use seamlessly. And customers can use applications in addition to Windows services through Azure. In particular, Azure's hybrid cloud makes it possible to connect private data centers and public clouds within the enterprise, allowing the use of integrated data without complicated procedures. Data centers have been established in 34 regions (as of July 2017) worldwide, and continuous and smooth operation is possible. Similar to AWS, users can flexibly adjust their resource usage, and users only pay for the resources they use. For this reason, MS Azure is leading the

---

[6] *Like Netflix, the number of customers who connect to Amazon.com to purchase goods and services and transaction volumes vary greatly depending on the season. Amazon is having tremendous success by going beyond solving their own problems and modeling a service called the cloud.*

[7] *Based on its strong market share with products such as Microsoft Windows and Office, the market share was increased by emphasizing the advantages and compatibility of Azure cloud introduction to customers who use existing products. The strength of the MS cloud is that customers can use their existing products in an optimal environment.*

cloud market along with Amazon, and new data centers continue to expand to regions around the world.

3.11 Overlook – Cloud

Thanks to the transformation from a traditional model to the cloud, the computer environment we use has changed drastically. We can see the future of the cloud via the market value of the companies that provide cloud services and go public. CrowdStrike (an endpoint protection cybersecurity[8] company) and SnowFlake (a cloud-based enterprise datawarehouse[9] company) show a high corporate value that exceeds expectations after the public offering. Enterprise services such as security monitoring, enterprise data storage space, and enterprise resource management systems, and personal entertainment services such as music streaming (Spotify, etc.) and movie-streaming services (Netflix), are moving to cloud environments. There is no disagreement even among experts on the transition to the cloud across all areas. In addition, the market will grow accordingly, and specialists will continue to be needed. It is expected that the cloud will evolve into a new form through the convergence of other 4th Industrial Revolution technologies.

Table 3.3. Emerging Cloud Service Providers

Company	Service
CrowdStrike	Endpoint security
DataDog	Security monitoring
DocuSign	Electronic signature and agreement cloud
Fastly	Content delivery network
The Trade Desk	Demand-side platform
Twilio	Cloud communications platform
Zoom Video Communications	Virtual conference & communication platform
zScaler	Security monitoring

---

[8] *Unlike the method of installing and using antivirus software on individual computers in the past, the endpoint protection security method is a SaaS type cloud service that installs only a simple sensor on each computer and monitors the security status on a cloud server.*
[9] *Datawarehouse refers to a storage space in which data from multiple data sources are collected in one place for report writing in a company. In the past, companies built and managed their own data warehouses. SnowFlake has a business in the form of building these data warehouses in the cloud, providing them to companies and receiving service fees.*

CHAPTER 4

BIG DATA

4.1 What Is Big Data?

Although the term *big data* is a buzzword these days, it is not easy to come up with a single definition for it. A large amount of data itself may be called big data, but in general, it is desirable to understand that big data is a series of processes from the beginning of data to the end of use, such as data collection, processing, storage, and analysis. This is because the technologies introduced earlier, such as the IoT, cloud computing, and artificial intelligence, are inevitably related to big data. In the past, the data collection method consisted mainly of collecting data planned by government agencies or a small number of companies,[1] whereas current data collection is collected in real time from mobile devices or the IoT and stored and analyzed in cloud computing space. This becomes possible because the infrastructure that can accomplish this has been established. This process is indeed expanding from the field of consumer behavior analytics to the production process, in which the efficiency of production is closely monitored in advance by various machine learning algorithms in real time through a vast amount of data collected by various sensors. In summary, big data can be understood as a series of processes that provide insights to achieve the user's goal. In other words, in the flood of countless data, valuable information is extracted to establish a knowledge system, and wisdom is obtained from this.

---

[1] *This kind of traditional data collection is more time-consuming, which leads to the low level of data frequency.*

The most important characteristics of big data can be summarized as the 5Vs, which are as follows:

1. Volume

2. Variety

3. Velocity

4. Veracity

5. Value

In terms of data volume, it can be said that the size of the amount of data generated on the earth has increased exponentially due to the spread of the Internet and smartphones. It is estimated that 90% of the existing data has been made over the past 2–3 years. When each reader closely observes their daily lives, they will be able to grasp how much data they are producing.

In terms of data variety, the types of data we can use have also rapidly expanded. While in the past, relational data in the form of data tables composed of numbers was mainly used for analysis, many forms of data sets including text data, image data, audio data, video data, and so on are now used for this purpose. A representative example is the "voice phishing prevention" app service. The "Phishing Stop" service jointly developed by the Financial Supervisory Service of Korea and Industrial Bank provides a service that distinguishes whether the incoming call is phishing or not through a model based on actual voice phishing voice data. While the strategy in the past focused on the campaign for phishing prevention, the current strategy is changing into a direct intervention that determines whether the voice phishing is voice phishing, as it is possible to secure related voice data and analyze it.

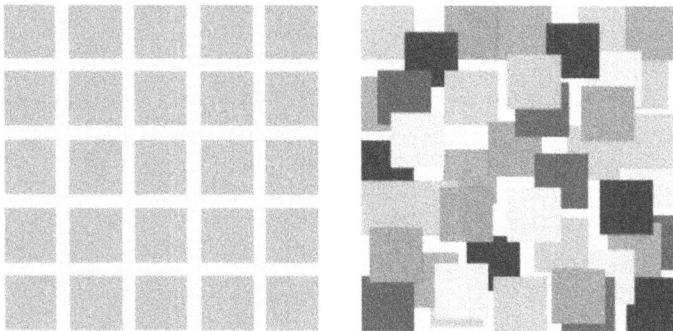

FIGURE 4.1. Structured data versus unstructured data.

In terms of data generation speed, various types of data are being generated in real time at a speed that is incomparable to the past. With the development of the IoT, mobile devices, information and communication technologies, and the spread of cloud computing, the cost of storing and analyzing data generated in real time is dramatically decreasing.

In terms of data veracity, big data is different from traditional data. Compared to traditional data, the amount and type of data are so vast that the quality of data cannot be assured. In the case of data provided by government agencies or a small number of companies in the past, the pre-process of verifying the quality of the data through several steps had been performed by these parties. However, in the case of big data, the consistency and quality of the data cannot be guaranteed. Therefore, in analyzing big data, it can be said that the most important task is to properly process and manage noise inherently embedded in the data.

Lastly, the significance of big data analytics exists only when value can be created through big data. In South Korea, many companies introduced big data analysis techniques into business without any clear purpose. For this reason, many big data-based business projects have failed. This is also the result of the introduction of big data into business models without a detailed plan for the areas where big data analysis is needed and the direction of use. Data has existed in the past, and data will continue to exist in the future, but the work of finding value and gaining insights from data is not done. This applies not only to the big data domain but to all data analysis. The value that big data analysis can bring will be maximized only when preceded by clear and concrete recognition of areas that cannot be solved with existing data and analysis tools.

4.2 Purpose of Big Data Analytics

Depending on the target and area to be analyzed, the purpose of big data analysis may differ in detail, but the purpose of big data analytics can be generally summarized as follows.

- First, processing the analysis target itself to be able to understand and explain

- Second, to predict the future through past data

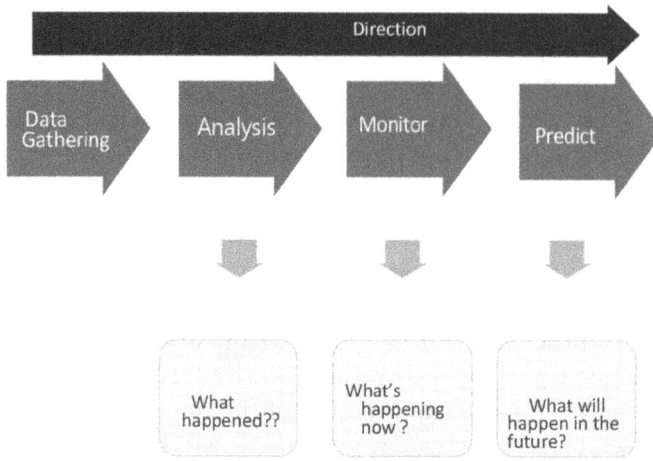

FIGURE 4.2. Development phase of data analytics.

For the first purpose, mentioned previously, we aim to effectively extract significant information about an analysis target from a sea of numerous data called big data. For example, from a corporate marketing point of view, it meets this purpose when trying to establish a marketing strategy by classifying similar types of consumers based on the structured and unstructured data of numerous customers. In other words, it is possible to classify individual customers into clusters and develop promotional activities specialized for that group. Also, it can be said that data analysis conducted in this context discovers common factors that can well capture the characteristics of the analysis target in big data consisting of hundreds of thousands of variables.

The second purpose of big data analytics is to predict what will happen in the future based on the available data. The subject of prediction may differ from field to field. For example, in the medical field, it can be used to predict in advance whether a specific tumor is a malignant or benign tumor based on the patient's MRI image data. In the economic field, the future changes of major economic indicators (e.g., GDP growth rate, stock price index, exchange rate) can be subjects for prediction. In the banking sector, big data can be used to predict whether a borrower will default in the future. The fields of application are endless. The prediction using big data is analogous to the search for the specific form of the function, that is, the specific form of F, which makes it possible to accurately predict Y (prediction target), which is our interest, with the data (X) given in the following equation.

$$Y_{t+1} = F(X_t)$$

In the case of big data analysis for prediction, the accuracy of prediction becomes the most important concern, and methods to increase the predictive power are closely related to artificial intelligence/machine learning, which is described in the next chapter. In other words, new data is accumulated in real time, and learning continues to occur to improve the accuracy of prediction. This point is what makes a big difference between traditional data analysis and big data analysis. In big data analysis, it is not meaningful to explain the past data well, and the most important issue is how to accurately predict the future based on currently available data. For example, suppose we have data on coronavirus patient information as shown in the following table.[2]

Table 4.1. Coronavirus Infected Patients Hypothetical Data

Patient Serial Number	Gender	Age	Presence of Underlying Disease	Status
1000000001	male	50	Y	Deceased
1000000002	male	30	N	Released
1000000003	male	50	N	Released
1000000004	male	20	N	Released
1000000005	female	20	Y	Deceased
1000000006	female	50	Y	Released
1000000007	male	20	N	Released
1000000008	male	20	N	Released

The core goal of coronavirus-related big data analysis can be summarized as predicting in advance whether it will lead to a serious or death event given the information of the patient, which makes it easier for us to come up with an appropriate treatment or intervention in advance. Of course, from a medical point of view, it is possible to judge whether it develops into severe illness or death, but it is also possible from the point of view of big data analysis. In other words, after constructing a learning model that can predict the possibility of death based on various information (e.g., age, presence of underlying disease, region, gender, etc.) on coronavirus infected patients, the degree of risk can be predicted in advance for newly infected patients. As the information on the virus-infected person accumulates over time, the

---

[2] *Of course, the actual related data will be data containing more variables and confirmed cases. The tables presented in the text are processed data for explanation.*

predictive model can be modified in real time, and the learning model can evolve in the direction of increasing prediction accuracy.

4.3 Big Data Analytics-Related Technology Solutions

Compared to past data, big data is overwhelmingly large in terms of size and diversity, so there is a limit to handling it with traditional analysis tools. Therefore, in the process of big data analysis, there is no choice but to form an ecosystem where technologies in various fields interact with each other. The general flow of big data analysis can be expressed as shown in the following figure, and detailed technologies play a role in each step.

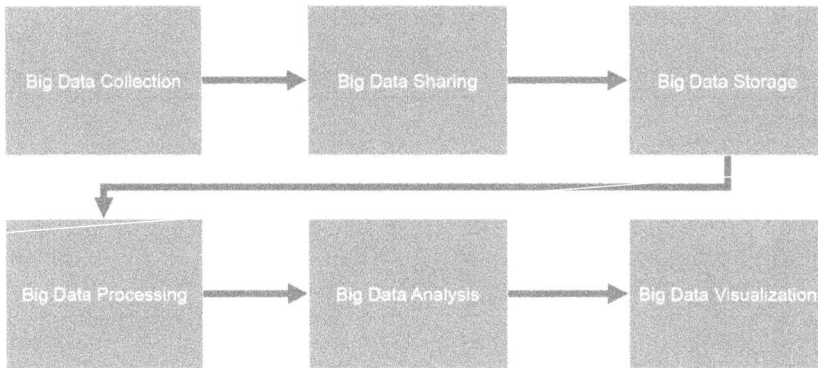

FIGURE 4.3. Flow of big data analytics.

1. Data collection: it refers to the act of actively collecting data on the target of analysis. The IoT and web crawling algorithms are used to collect online data.

2. Data storage: it is no exaggeration to say that the development of Hadoop has made big data analysis easier. The Hadoop system is a system that can process large amounts of data at a low cost and has established itself as a standard platform (Java-based open-source framework) for big data processing. Hadoop is a free solution that provides a service that stores and processes large amounts of data by integrating multiple computers into one. It stores data in thousands of distributed storage devices and distributed computing devices.

3. Analysis and visualization: Splunk, a big data analysis solution competitor of Hadoop, provides machine data (various servers, networks, IoT

equipment, and various sources) through a web-based interface. It is a representative solution that provides a real-time distributed computing platform that can collect, store, analyze, visualize applications, and so on. It has the function to collect and process even unstructured data including text and voice regardless of the format and capacity of the data, and it is a solution that enables the overall function of big data processing without complicated coding or the help of external solutions.

4.4 Big Data Application Business Cases

In this section, we are going to introduce some business applications of big data. Existing and potential business applications of big data are not limited to materials covered in this section. Also, the way big data is applied to a business may vary depending on the firm's business strategies and the industry structure in which the firm operates.

4.4.1 Amazon Inc.

Amazon Inc., a world-class e-commerce company, provides a cloud-based solution (AWS) that enables big data analysis for other companies, while also providing effective inventory management and data analysis of its customers. It can be said to be an iconic company that led to an increase in sales using big data analytics. The data Amazon collects is not limited to just the data left behind by customers online. For example, in the case of AmazonGo, an unmanned store operated by Amazon, customers can directly visit the store to purchase products, and the sensors and cameras installed in the store allow customers to see how they act in physically existing stores. Data about customer actions (e.g., which products are carefully examined) are also collected and used to analyze customers' purchasing behavior. Such information is used to establish a meaningful marketing strategy by combining various information about customers (race, age, gender, etc.). Purchase patterns of online customers are also subject to collection and analysis.

In addition, in the case of e-commerce companies, efficient inventory management has a great influence on profitability. According to the analysis of data on the purchasing behavior of users, it promotes inventory exhaustion through discount promotions and efficient geographical distribution of inventory products through prediction of purchasing patterns.

FIGURE 4.4. AmazonGo Store (Source: Creative Commons).

4.4.2 Starbucks

Starbucks, which started out as a small coffee shop in Seattle, has grown into a global coffee chain company over the past 30 years. There may be many factors for Starbucks's success, but big data is evaluated as contributing to Starbucks's growth. In the case of coffee stores, their geographic location has a great influence on the sales of the store, and Starbucks is known to have made a thorough data-based decision on the business district in the area when entering a new area. In other words, it is known that decisions about the optimal location are made based on the analysis of various data on the relevant commercial area, such as the floating population, traffic volume, and population of the corresponding area. When Starbucks enters a new commercial district, the store location is selected by estimating the impact on other Starbucks stores in the vicinity. In addition to selecting the location of the store, new menu development and menu recommendations are made based on data on customers collected from Starbucks-only applications.

4.4.3 Netflix

Netflix is a global company that supplies various media content online. In the early days, it started a business that sold or rented DVDs by mail, but in

2010, it entered the online market and transformed into a data-based media content streaming company. Netflix's own movies and dramas, as well as various movies and drama shows, are provided in a streaming method. From the point of online business, Netflix made it possible to collect data on users, and in the end, a "recommendation function" based on customer behavior data, which is the core technology of Internet TV, became possible. As many people consume media content through Netflix, it is possible to acquire microscopic data on what genre of content people consume at what time. Based on this data, recommending optimized media content to customers and making users continue to subscribe to Netflix is a way for Netflix to continuously generate revenue. The recommendation algorithm that Netflix is using is the result of big data such as data accumulated by Netflix users around the world, evaluation of media content, and subscription patterns.

4.4.4 Bank of America

Bank of America is a representative company that uses big data from an all-around view of business operations. Bank of America's marketing strategy shifted its focus to "event-based marketing" based on user data analysis. No matter what channel (branch visit, online banking, etc.) the customer uses to contact the bank, Bank of America focuses on financial products (home mortgage loans, credit cards, etc.) that meet the customer's tendency and which they are likely to purchase. Therefore, when a customer visits a branch and consults with a bank employee, information about the financial product most attractive to the customer is automatically transmitted, and the bank employee can conduct marketing activities based on this information. The main feature of the product group by consumer customization is that it maintains consistency no matter which channel the customer uses.

In terms of risk management, the use of big data has significantly reduced the tangible and intangible costs of banks. Financial companies regularly calculate the default probability for borrowers. Instead of estimating the risk of a loan portfolio according to the default probability by relying on an external probability prediction model provided as in the past, a dedicated computing platform based on parallel computing was introduced. This reduced the time to calculate the risk of a portfolio of more than 100 million loan accounts from 96 hours to 1 hour. This shift allows banks to achieve higher efficiencies in terms of risk management and enables faster decision-making.

4.4.5 IBM Watson Health

The medical industry is regarded as a representative field in which the potential of big data can be maximized. The use of big data is expected to promote hospital operation efficiency, accurate diagnosis, and reduction of medical costs. IBM's Watson Health is a company that provides a representative data analysis platform service in the medical field.

The Watson Health system provides various options and guidelines for the cause of the disease and the appropriate treatment method for a specific patient based on the vast amount of data related to a specific disease (information on other patients in the past, medical papers, medical textbooks, pharmaceutical information). The Watson Health system is an artificial intelligence-based system, and learning was done from doctors in actual medical institutions.

If a patient is diagnosed with cancer, the doctor who treats it simply registers medical information about the patient in the system and, based on the vast amount of data on the disease accumulated by Watson Health, the doctor is provided the appropriate treatment method for the patient. Watson Health can be said to be a big data analysis service with very high accessibility because it can be operated on doctors' smartphones or tablets.

4.4.6 RegTech

RegTech is a compound word combining Regulation and Technology. It utilizes information and communication technology (ICT) to streamline regulatory compliance, compliance monitoring, and operational risk management granted by regulatory authorities of companies (financial companies). It can be defined as a set of data-driven services that enable firms to do regulatory compliance easier. In the case of Quantex, based on a wide range of customer data (including data on human networks between customers) held by financial companies, Quantex supports the operation of financial companies related to money laundering prevention based on artificial intelligence. It provides a service that reflects the various transaction records of customers taking place in the market in real-time analysis.

4.5 The Future of Big Data

As emphasized in the preface, data collected from various sources will play a key role in creating value for the future economic system. In other words, it is not an exaggeration to see that the 4th Industrial Revolution is a kind of data revolution. In many business areas, big data analysis is expected to play a leading role in the development of new business models and services, as well as a secondary role in the process of strategy establishment and decision-making. We think it will play an important role in bridging the gap between the unsatisfied demand of consumers and supply ability between suppliers, a problem that existing business models cannot solve.

Until now, big data analysis has been widely used in the marketing domain through consumer behavior analysis based on the digital footprints of users formed on interconnected networks. However, just because there is a lot of data does not always guarantee there will be good results, and on the contrary, it cannot be said that a small amount of data brings bad results. The added value that big data analysis can bring may vary depending on the nature of the problem to be solved in individual business sites and the goals pursued. Therefore, it is necessary to adopt big data analysis according to the nature of the business and the characteristics of the application field.

Besides, some worry about the alienation of humans from the labor market due to the big data revolution. In other words, human labor can be rapidly replaced in some occupations due to the automation of processes or office processing through artificial intelligence. For example, many companies have introduced a "chatbot," which is a trend in which computer algorithms play the role of customer service.[3] Despite this trend, it will be difficult to replace all areas of the business scene with robots or artificial intelligence-based algorithms. This is because humans will eventually be responsible for designing the algorithm's infrastructure, and humans will eventually be responsible for interpreting the results of data analysis and gaining insights from it. Therefore, to successfully prepare for the era of the 4th Industrial Revolution, it is necessary to have the ability to collect, process, and analyze various types of data, as well as have insight into the business environment and changes in consumer behavior.

---

[3] *To increase the work efficiency of the chatbot, learning must take place based on the previously established data related to customer service.*

CHAPTER 5

ARTIFICIAL INTELLIGENCE AND MACHINE LEARNING

5.1 Artificial Intelligence Is Now Deeply Infiltrated into Everyday Life

We already live with the phrase artificial intelligence in modern society. When did we begin to hear this term so often? Many will remember the competition of AlphaGo and Sedol Lee in 2016. This exciting battle of the century has made artificial intelligence a big topic in the world. When artificial intelligence defeated Sedol Lee, the world was amazed. Even those who did not know much about artificial intelligence realized how advanced artificial intelligence was to have reached the level of surpassing humans. Swept by this current, numerous products and services using artificial intelligence have been released globally, and the era has arrived in which the phrase artificial intelligence is familiarly heard through various media. Now, artificial intelligence is deeply positioned in our daily lives.

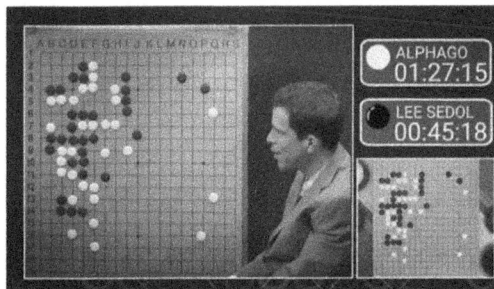

FIGURE 5.1. Match of AlphaGo and Lee Sedol (source: "8:36pm Match 3 of AlphaGo vs Lee Sedol. The confidence of the human commentary is fascinating" by Buster Benson is licensed under CC BY-SA 2.0).

Many people access their smartphone devices dozens of times a day using their smartphone's face recognition function. Artificial intelligence is also embedded in these technologies, which have become a part of everyday life. Apple's Face ID scans a user's face with more than 30,000 dots and stores the data. Through this, whether the scanned face matches the registered face is calculated and compared at high speed. In this case, artificial intelligence is used to judge face recognition. So, how can artificial intelligence be able to recognize faces smartly and quickly? This performance is made possible by a process called "training." In Apple's face recognition using artificial intelligence, artificial intelligence was trained with 1 billion face samples. Due to this vast amount of data, Apple's face recognition has reached the level of naturally recognizing faces when users simply glance at their phones. This is just one example, and artificial intelligence is already deeply permeating our everyday products, including speakers, vacuum cleaners, and even air conditioners. We experience artificial intelligence in products and services every day, but it is not easy to quickly define it. Let us now briefly consider its definition.

5.2 What Is Artificial Intelligence?

If you interpret artificial intelligence literally, it can be said that it is an artificial implementation of human intelligence. It is no exaggeration to say that the concept of artificial intelligence has been latent from the time we invented computers. From the time computers were created until now, we have been trying to make smarter computers. Going further, we want computers to do things with human-like intelligence. Such computers are called artificial intelligence computers. Artificial intelligence computers can automate what humans do, make decisions independently, and interact with humans like humans. In modern society, with the help of artificial intelligence, humans can be guaranteed a more convenient life, and artificial intelligence brings enormous cost savings to companies through fast and accurate processing.

As artificial intelligence develops further in the future, emotions and love similar to humans will be felt, and sympathy and relationships with humans and AIs may be formed. In the case of Naoki Urasawa's cartoon *Pluto*, the robot is raised to a level where it is difficult to tell the difference from humans when viewed with the naked eye due to a very advanced artificial intelligence. These highly developed robots can marry and love, and even weep when a loved one is lost. At the moment, it sounds like a story only in cartoons, but what this story implies is that artificial intelligence has several classifications depending on the degree of development. From now on, let us look at the types of artificial intelligence.

5.3 Are There Types of Artificial Intelligence?

As mentioned earlier that artificial intelligence is an artificial implementation of human intelligence. Such artificial intelligence can be divided into several types according to the level of intelligence. In other words, there are three types in theory as seen in Table 5.1.

Table 5.1. Three Different Types of Artificial Intelligence

Artificial Intelligence Type	Characteristics
Weak artificial intelligence	Machines can learn and judge for clearly defined tasks.
Strong artificial intelligence	Machines think and solve problems independently.
Super artificial intelligence	Machines have intelligence far beyond the human.

5.3.1 Weak Artificial Intelligence

Weak artificial intelligence can be understood as literally "weak" artificial intelligence. This type of artificial intelligence has a narrow range of thinking, and examples are the products and services that make up the majority of our lives. For example, a robot cleaner equipped with artificial intelligence can distinguish between human feet and thresholds. Artificial intelligence learns the shape of a vast amount of human feet through the camera and radar sensors of the vacuum cleaner, and when human feet appear during actual cleaning, they wait or avoid them. The level of intelligence of such artificial intelligence is sometimes evaluated as the level of "ape," "child," or "dolphin." In other words, this weak artificial intelligence can learn and judge for clearly defined tasks. However, it is still limited compared to the level of intelligence and the scope of application of thinking of humans. Then, in the case of strong artificial intelligence, how much more advanced is it than weak artificial intelligence?

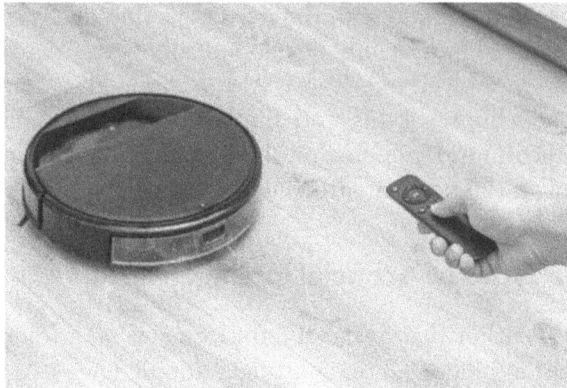

FIGURE 5.2. Artificial intelligence robotic vacuum cleaner (source: "Close-up of a man holding remote control of robotic vacuum cleaner to start cleaning" by wuestenigel is licensed under CC BY 2.0).

5.3.2 Strong Artificial Intelligence

Strong artificial intelligence is a "strong" artificial intelligence that allows computers and machines to think and solve problems independently. What is even more surprising is that machines have the perceptual ability to recognize themselves and can continue to evolve on their own. It can be seen that it is a distinctly evolved form compared to the previous examples of weak artificial intelligence. Then, can we find examples of such strong artificial intelligence around us? In movies, cartoons, science fiction, and so forth, we have already encountered it. For example, Samantha, artificial intelligence in the movie *Her*, communicates with the protagonist and falls in love. In other words, it is possible for her to understand human emotions and to have a real conversation. Samantha, such a strong artificial intelligence, is tough to implement realistically. For example, artificial intelligence must accumulate and learn memories and experiences with users over time, and through them, they must be able to melt into daily conversations naturally. However, robots that exist today use a similar form of questions and greetings every day, "Hello. What can I do for you?" It is also necessary to be able to effectively determine which psychological state the user is in by analyzing various factors such as the user's language, facial expressions, and gestures. For artificial intelligence to implement behavioral patterns such as the formation of humans' natural intimacy, many variables and vast amounts of data must be considered. If so, will there be robots or software that go beyond these movies' content and realize the level of strong artificial intelligence in the present world?

Currently, Watson, developed by IBM, is said to be the closest thing to strong artificial intelligence. In 2011, Watson showed his high level of artificial intelligence as he beat humans overwhelmingly in the famous American quiz show *Jeopardy*. How far has Watson evolved since then? Watson has also expanded into the medical field. When Watson was introduced to University Hospital for cancer diagnosis, people had great expectations that Watson could replace or exceed existing doctors. However, as a result of the actual application, the rate of consensus between Watson and the doctor was not higher than expected, and IBM gradually turned away from the medical industry. Judging from these cases, it seems that there is still a lot of homework to be done to reach strong artificial intelligence. In this current situation, it can be expected that super artificial intelligence, the last kind of artificial intelligence, is only possible in theory. Let us look at the difference between super artificial intelligence and strong artificial intelligence.

FIGURE 5.3. IBM Watson in the *Jeopardy* quiz show (source: "Don't call me Watson. That's not my name." by charliecurve is licensed under CC BY-SA 2.0)

5.3.3 Super Artificial Intelligence

It is expected that super artificial intelligence will have intelligence and thinking far exceeding humans in an evolved form from strong artificial intelligence. This means that it can be positioned as a threat to humans. These concerns have also been cited by Stephen Hawking, Bill Gates, and Elon Musk. For example, it will completely replace human jobs, or machines with strong aggression will potentially dominate humans. In the movie *Terminator Genisys*, the artificial intelligence program recognizes humans as enemies and tries to destroy humans by producing robots. An artificial intelligence designed by humans could destroy humanity. This is called the singularity of technology.

In other words, the evolution of artificial intelligence is so rapid that it becomes difficult to predict the future. About 100 years ago, airplanes were first created by the Wright brothers, but now humanity has reached the level of conquering Mars. Given these technologies' exponential growth, it may not be impossible to create super artificial intelligence within the next 50 years. Then, how can artificial intelligence be effectively controlled so that it can be compatible with humans? There are also predictions that it will not be easy to control super artificial intelligence because it is far ahead of humans. If so, should we not proceed with the development of super artificial intelligence itself? It is not easy to find the correct answer at this time. Whether the birth of super artificial intelligence will provide humanity with a different level of life or whether it will be the greatest threat to human extinction, no one knows yet, and it can be said to be an essential task for humanity. From now on, let us take a look at how artificial intelligence, which exerts significant influence on our modern and future society, has been created and developed.

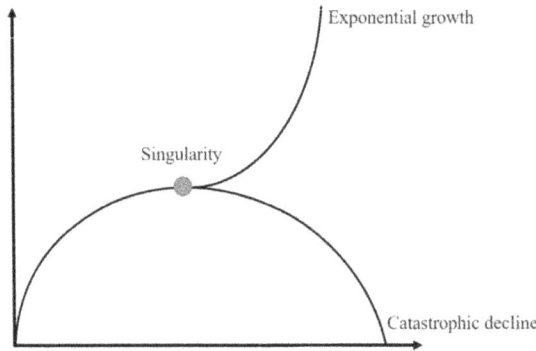

FIGURE 5.4. The singularity point of artificial intelligence technology.

5.4 How Has Artificial Intelligence Developed?

Although artificial intelligence has a relatively short history, it exerts great influence on the present and future society. When did the concept of artificial intelligence emerge? Around 1950, a thesis by British mathematician Alan Turing marked the beginning of artificial intelligence history. In his thesis, "Computing Machinery and Intelligence," he argued that if the computer's reaction cannot be distinguished from the human reaction, the computer has the intelligence to think for itself.[1] He also predicted that in the 2000s, 50 years later, it would be possible for humans to talk in text and then not notice that they had conversations with machines. This interesting concept stimulated many later scientists' challenges, and scientists devised more specific experimental methods, and these experiments called "Turing tests" were named after him.

Let us look at a more specific experimental method of the Turing test. The referee enters a room with two computers. Humans manipulate one computer, and the computer itself controls the rest. Of course, the referee does not know which one is controlled by humans, and they communicate with each computer through text chat. Chatting takes place for 5 minutes each, and the referee decides that the person with whom the conversation took place more naturally is human and makes a choice. At this time, if more than 30% of the judges mistake the conversation with the computer as human, it is recognized as having artificial intelligence. What have been the results of these interesting experiments? Surprisingly, passing these Turing tests was a huge barrier for scientists, and for a long time no one passed them.

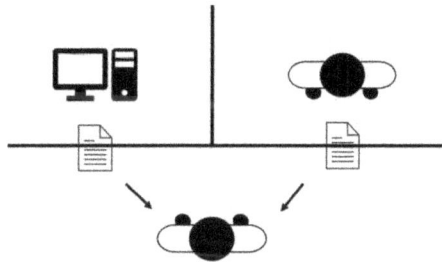

FIGURE 5.5. The Turing test.

Then, in 2014, a computer that passed the Turing test for the first time 65 years after Alan Turing's theory became known to the world appeared. The computer was named Eugene Goostman. Eugene Goostman, a 13-year-old boy living in Ukraine, first introduced himself as not speaking English as his first language, and 33% of the 25 referees mistook Eugene Goostman as a human being. Many people praised the artificial intelligence that passed the Turing test for the first time, but some expressed skepticism that Eugene Goostman was a simple chat robot. There were criticisms that the proper evaluation had to be limited because it was set as a 13-year-old boy speaking

---

[1] *Turing, Alan M. "Computing machinery and intelligence." Parsing the turing test. Springer, Dordrecht, 2009. 23–65.*

in English rather than his mother tongue. Returning to Alan Turing's concept of artificial intelligence, the ability to "think for ourselves" must be built into machines. If you go out of the Turing test and talk to Eugene Goostman every day comfortably, it would be unreasonable to feel that Eugene Goostman is human. From this point of view, it can be seen that implementing human-like dialogue goes beyond improving the computer's memory and computational functions and requires a deeper consideration of what human thinking ability is. Although it was a controversial result, it can be appreciated that the Turing test provided a field of opportunity for many scientists to consider the definition of human thinking and the methodology for implementing it.

5.5 Artificial Intelligence, Machine Learning, Deep Learning

So far, we have looked at the concept and development process of artificial intelligence. In addition to artificial intelligence, you may have heard the terms machine learning or deep learning. So, what is the relationship between machine learning and deep learning and artificial intelligence? Machine learning and deep learning can be seen as sub-concepts of artificial intelligence. More precisely, the sub-concept of artificial intelligence is machine learning, and the sub-concept of machine learning is deep learning. Let us take a closer look at machine learning first.

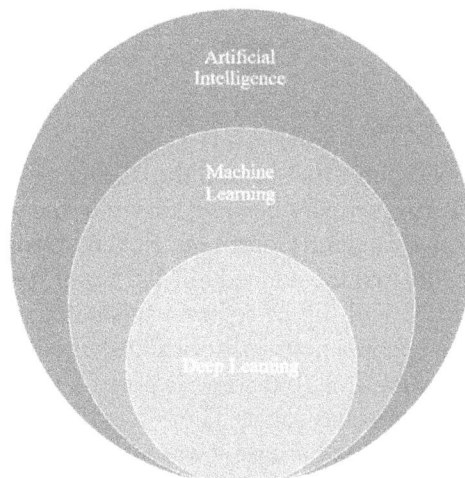

FIGURE 5.6. Artificial intelligence, machine learning, and deep learning relationships.

Machine learning is a sub-concept of artificial intelligence and can be seen as one of the concrete approaches to realizing artificial intelligence. In other words, it learns data through an algorithm, and through this, it makes judgments and predictions about new situations. Let us take a simple example. If you use a music player from time to time, you may have experienced a surprise because the recommended music matches your taste. So how does a music player recommend music? Similar songs will likely be recommended based on data such as personal history or listening list. Machine learning goes further and analyzes the sound source's signal to provide users with more diverse and accurate recommended songs. For example, the sound source signal (time, frequency) is split and other patterns such as vocals, keyboards, drums, and guitars are pulled out, which are then numerically analyzed. If the song's numerical value that the user likes and the song analyzed are similar, the corresponding sound source is recommended. This way, it takes only about 3 seconds to analyze one song, so you can explore a lot of the latest songs without difficulty. So, is machine learning the only way to develop artificial intelligence?

Before machine learning became popular, the primary development method of artificial intelligence was programming. In other words, it was a knowledge-processing work method in which rules were defined in advance based on human knowledge and passed along with data in an easy-to-understand method (a combination of symbols). But machine learning takes a different approach. When humans provide data and results, the computer learns and discovers common properties and patterns based on them. In a way, programming is a form of injectable education, and machine learning is a form of self-learning. So, what advantages does this machine learning have over conventional programming?

Machine learning can figure out the rules through self-learning without humans' need to develop complex formulas and rules (programming). For example, suppose the problem is to classify human walking and running only through speed data. If we approach conventional programming, humans will have to establish the relationship between speed, walking, and running with a formula. At first glance, creating such a relationship as a formula seems simple. Still, it is not an easy task because it considers various variables such as individual health status, age, and surrounding environment (wind, road surface). Perhaps hundreds or even thousands of lines of code are required to produce accurate results.

Let us assume that this is approached using machine learning. Initially, you will need speed data for hundreds or thousands of people walking and running in various environments. However, when a sufficient amount of data is accumulated, machine learning can recognize the difference between walking and running individuals and learn how walking and running change in the surrounding environment. In particular, as more and more data are accumulated in machine learning, learning ability increases and more accurate judgments can be made. In this way, machine learning deviates from the existing programming methods and presents a new problem-solving method that is more dependent on data. So, what is the difference between deep learning and machine learning?

FIGURE 5.7. Walking and running examples.

Deep learning is a sub-concept of machine learning and can be said to be a system that learns through numerous simulations and trial and error. At this time, reinforcement learning is carried out mainly based on an artificial neural network. So, first, what is an artificial neural network? An artificial neural network refers to an algorithm created to work like a human brain by imitating human learning methods. A large amount of data is also required for proper learning.

Let us try to understand the basic principles of artificial neural networks with an easy example. Suppose that a circle and triangle are separated through an artificial neural network. At this time, the artificial neural network's input layer receives the input data, and the output layer calculates the predicted value. There is a hidden layer between the input layer and the output layer, from one layer to several layers, that is responsible for most of the computational functions. When a circle picture is given as data, each pixel value constituting the circle is input to the input layer nodes. The input layer is then connected to the hidden layer, and weights are calculated in this process. Here, we find out which nodes are more active by the computational process. The activated nodes selected in this way are connected to the next hidden layer again to operate, and finally, probability values for circles and triangles are output.

But this is not the end. Suppose that the actual circle is output as a triangle by mistake by the artificial neural network. In this case, a correction value is presented to reduce such an error according to the degree of the difference between the predicted value and the actual value. This learning process proceeds to backward propagation in the network. This forward propagation and backward propagation are repeated countless times, and the circle is actually identified with a high probability. Then, returning to the original question, what is the difference between machine learning and deep learning?

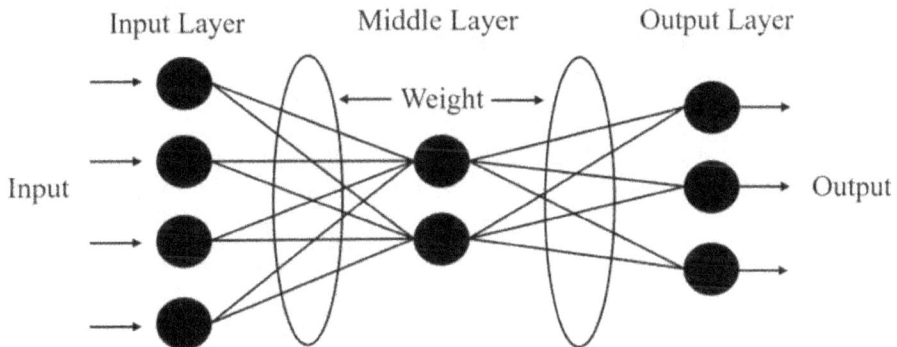

FIGURE 5.8 Artificial neural network example.

To understand the difference between machine learning and deep learning, let us use an example of classifying dog and cat images. Suppose your goal is to see images of dogs and cats like humans and accurately identify them. First, how can humans distinguish between dogs and cats? There are dozens of hundreds of dogs and cats, respectively, and various forms exist within the same species. Perhaps when you show a small child several pictures of dogs and cats, they may not distinguish them properly in some cases. It can be said that humans unconsciously see countless dogs and cats in their lives, and these accumulated experiences further enhance their ability to distinguish between dogs and cats. So, can the same logic be applied to machines? When you show the machine countless pictures of dogs and cats, can the machine finally make it clear?

FIGURE 5.9. Cats and dogs example.

Here, machine learning and deep learning use different approaches to reach the goal. In the case of machine learning, human intervention is required first. For example, humans can mark specific areas such as cat whiskers and dog noses that characterize each dog and cat picture, and machine learning helps them learn. This procedure is called "labeling." Based on this learning, machine learning determines whether an individual or a cat is looking at a new image. This method is called supervised learning.

So, how is the deep learning method different? The main difference is that unsupervised learning, which excludes human intervention, is possible. In other words, in the case of deep learning, depending on the nature of the problem, it can be applied to supervised and unsupervised learning problems. In this example, we will focus on the unsupervised learning of deep learning. In using the unsupervised learning of deep learning, pictures of dogs and cats are provided as input data without prior human work (marking specific areas of dogs and cats). At this time, deep learning is to determine which types of dogs and cats can be distinguished through numerous trials and errors. To distinguish between cats and dogs without human assistance, a computer with vast amounts of learning data and high computational power is required compared to machine learning methods. Also, it is often difficult to understand how accurate results are derived because the calculation process is black-boxed due to a complex calculation model.

These deep learning methods sometimes lead to creative results that are very different from humans. In some cases, easy problems for humans are difficult, or, conversely, problems that are difficult for humans are easily solved. As an interesting example, it once became a hot topic because deep learning could not differentiate between chocolate muffins and Chihuahua photos. From now on, let us take a closer look at the case of AlphaGo, which has spread deep learning to the public.

5.6 Deep Learning Technology That Composes AlphaGo

AlphaGo and Sedol Lee's competition was a historical event where you could feel at a glance how far the development of deep learning came. First of all, why did DeepMind, the company that developed AlphaGo, choose Go as the main target? The reason lies in the complexity of Go. In the case of chess, the movement method and value of each piece are determined, but there is no such limitation in the case of Go. For this reason, the number of cases where the Go stone can be placed is 10 to the power of 170, which is said to be equivalent to the number of atoms in the entire universe. In the case of chess, while chess champion Kasparov was defeated by IBM's Deep Blue supercomputer in 1997, Go has long remained a challenge for artificial intelligence. Even before AlphaGo and Sedol Lee's game started, people expected Sedol Lee's overwhelming victory with 5-0. However, in the end, AlphaGo won 4-1 and shocked many people.

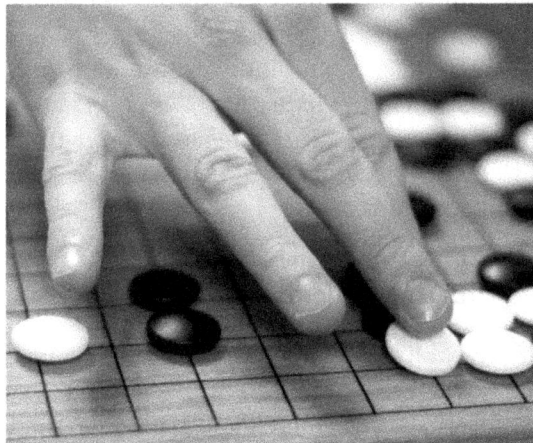

FIGURE 5.10. Example of playing Go (source: "placing the go stone" by luis de bethencourt is licensed under CC BY 2.0).

How could DeepMind train AlphaGo on the complex problem of Go? AlphaGo uses a new type of machine learning method that combines supervised learning and deep learning. In supervised learning, the position of stones on the board was questioned and the answers to possible numbers were labeled. AlphaGo is said to have learned 160,000 notations of Go and 30 million Go board data images. Through deep learning on this vast amount of data, it learned and improved how to choose numbers to win the game freely. In addition to that, AlphaGo has continuously improved its performance by playing "self-matching" with itself 1.28 million times. By playing Go on its own, it learned a number of more creative and new ways to escape the notation patterns of existing Go articles or humans. Interestingly, unlike human Go players who usually try to beat their opponents with a lot of house differences, AlphaGo learns strategies with only the goal of winning, whether the difference is small or big. Through this enormous number of games, AlphaGo learned the number of cases with a high probability of winning for each situation. AlphaGo is said to perform probability calculations based on big data and computational power equivalent to using 5,000 high-end computers at once for each number.

AlphaGo was not yet perfect. After Sedol Lee's 78th Go, AlphaGo continued to make mistakes and eventually lose in the fourth game. Through three games with AlphaGo, Sedol Lee came to understand the characteristics of AlphaGo to some extent, and the creative 78th Go, which was based on him, was difficult to predict even for AlphaGo, which was trained in the tremendous number of games. It can be said that the confrontation between AlphaGo and Sedol Lee showed a journey beyond the conflict between artificial intelligence and humans to understand each other. The 37th Go that led AlphaGo to victory in the second game was the creative play of complicated machines for humans to predict. The 78th Go that Sedol Lee showed afterward was the creative play of humans that artificial intelligence could not predict.

5.7 Are There Limits to Artificial Intelligence?

There are still several limitations to artificial intelligence. First, there is a substantial dependence on data. If an artificial intelligence learns terrible data for a long time, the artificial intelligence likely learned through it is also wrong. In a recent study, letting artificial intelligence resembling 5-year-old children learn with indiscriminate content has become a hot topic for spitting out slang or disregarding others. Also, since artificial intelligence learns and makes judgments by itself, a completely different artificial intelligence may be born that deviates from human development intentions at first. Like the movie *Terminator Genisys*, mentioned earlier, artificial intelligence may recognize humans as enemies.

Aside from that, bias can be planted in artificial intelligence. Human conscious or unconscious prejudice may permeate the data. Recently (as of April 2020), there was an anecdote about how Google apologized for its artificial intelligence making racist judgments. Google Vision AI recognized that a person with light skin was holding a thermometer, but if a person with dark skin was holding a thermometer, it was recognized as a gun. This is because an insufficient learning process, that is, unfair data, caused bias.

Finally, it is often difficult to know why artificial intelligence makes certain decisions. For example, there is an anecdote that YouTube had deleted twice as many videos as before since it started adjusting content with artificial intelligence, even though many of these deleted videos did not violate the rules. When asked about these mistakes, artificial intelligence cannot answer them, and it is often difficult for developers to know the cause. Artificial intelligence has both strengths and limitations. How is it applied to our modern society?

5.8 Artificial Intelligence Meets Business

First, artificial intelligence can be effectively applied in the marketing field. Performance can be optimized through artificial intelligence. Through machine learning algorithms, it is possible to quickly analyze a platform's ad performance and automate tasks, which can save time and money for performance analysis and improvement. Personalized advertisements can also be provided through artificial intelligence. Artificial intelligence can analyze individual customer behavior and make smart recommendations accordingly. For example, you may have experienced banner ads for products you are interested in appearing on social media web pages. These customized advertisements can be viewed as learning and prediction through artificial intelligence.

Artificial intelligence is also being actively applied in the healthcare field. Artificial intelligence can improve the efficiency of medical image analysis. For example, there are increasing cases in which automated analysis of artificial intelligence detects abnormal symptoms of body organs faster than humans. This automatic and precise analysis can bring about cost savings, and doctors can focus more on interpreting and resolving detected anomalies. Artificial intelligence can also be used in assisted robotic surgery. Artificial intelligence can help doctors who need surgical instruments in real time during surgery by learning and analyzing medical records data before surgery. Virtual nursing assistants based on artificial intelligence can effectively help patients. For example, Sensely's AI-powered nurse named "Molly" asks questions about a patient's health and evaluates symptoms. This automation can save money by saving the actual nurse's work time.

Artificial intelligence can also be applied in the field of employment. It is possible to find suitable candidates using artificial intelligence. Artificial intelligence learns and analyzes a massive amount of résumés to select candidates that meet the company's specifications. Candidate evaluation is also possible through artificial intelligence. Artificial intelligence learns the data of employees who have performed well in the past and evaluates whether candidates are comparable. Finally, candidate matching is also possible. Artificial intelligence comprehensively grasps information on the candidate's personal characteristics, skills, and desired annual salary to determine the required job's degree of suitability. The advantage of employing such artificial intelligence lies in its high efficiency. It takes a lot of time and human resources for humans to review the documents of numerous applicants. However, it takes an average of 3 seconds for the AI to evaluate the self-introduction letter. In 8 hours per day, 10,000 self-introductions can be evaluated.

Artificial intelligence is also widely applied in the financial field. First, it is possible to automate the work of financial companies through artificial intelligence. It can analyze documents, identify customers, and detect anomalies based on machine learning. U.S. investment bank JPMorgan Chase introduced the machine learning platform COiN (Contract Intelligence) to extract critical information and provisions from legal documents, resulting in innovative time and cost savings. Besides that, artificial intelligence can provide various services to financial customers. Machine learning-based chatbots are used to replace customer response tasks such as help desks and call centers. Japan's Mizuho Bank has introduced IBM's artificial intelligence Watson to perform customer response tasks with call centers, smartphone apps, and robots. Artificial intelligence is also used in credit rating systems. A more detailed credit evaluation is possible through machine learning by integrating and analyzing a customer's financial information and other information such as bill payment records, call records, and social network information. In particular, as the range of customers that can be analyzed through machine learning is increased, a more significant opportunity is given to those who have been unable to receive services due to a small financial record.

Finally, artificial intelligence can be used in various ways in the game field. Recently, in the arcade game (DOTA2), there was an anecdote that the game artificial intelligence (OpenAI) won a victory over a human expert team, including a former pro gamer. This showed the possibility of applying game artificial intelligence through deep learning, and research is underway to apply it to more complex games in the future. It is expected that it will be possible to produce intelligent game contents that adapt and evolve by themselves through artificial intelligence. In other words, the content of the game is changed according to the user's in-game behavior pattern and propensity. It is expected that it will be possible to experience creative and new content outside of the existing standardized game contents. Also, artificial intelligence is being used as a tool for analyzing game big data. There is an increasing demand for artificial intelligence to analyze users' log data information collected on a cloud basis and use it for management and marketing.

5.9 Our Attitude toward Future Artificial Intelligence

Finally, how is artificial intelligence changing now, and in what attitude should we embrace it? Will artificial intelligence be taking human jobs in the near future? You might come up with these questions. Perhaps machines are likely to replace humans in existing simple repetitive tasks due to automation and sensor technology. If so, there is a high possibility that humans will do more creative and high-thinking tasks that are difficult for artificial intelligence to do, that is, with little existing data. As a result, the importance of human-machine collaboration is likely to emerge. It is no surprise that humans and artificial intelligence work together in the workplace interactively. In distribution warehouses, humans are arranging objects more efficiently with artificial intelligence robots, and doctors are more accurately grasping diseases through the help of artificial intelligence. In other words, it can be seen that human work is not being eliminated due to defeat in the competition with artificial intelligence, but changes are occurring in humans' interactions with artificial intelligence.

These changes can have a significant impact not only on the job but also on students' curriculum. Education that requires simple information acquisition and memory is likely to be replaced by artificial intelligence, so curriculums that require more critical thinking and creativity should be treated more intensively. A curriculum suitable for this age of artificial intelligence will further cultivate students' ability to be compatible with artificial intelligence even after graduation. It will be essential for humans' ability and artificial intelligence to grow together in a relationship of harmony rather than confrontation.

CHAPTER 6

VIRTUAL AND AUGMENTED REALITY

6.1 New World Seen through the Lens

We live in the platform era, which began after the period of the 2000s when the manufacturing industry led the industrial ecosystem and is now in the period of the 4th Industrial Revolution. Global companies are trying to lead the industrial economy by building their platform in their way. When Apple's iPhone appeared in 2007, perceptions shifted from the existing IT platform, creating a new smartphone platform era. The iPhone completely changed the existing mobile phone concept and transformed it into a central device that is the condensation of all IT technologies.

Ten years have already passed since the era of smartphones. The IT platform has changed every ten years. The 1990s were the era of PC communication, the 2000s were the PC and web era, and the 2010s were the era of the smartphone and wireless Internet. What will be the leading role in the post-smartphone era?

Virtual reality and augmented reality are emerging as a powerhouse in the IT industry as new platforms. Beyond the existing smartphone-based content, the space of new experiences and dreams seen through lenses is becoming attractive to people. The concept of virtual/augmented reality has long been introduced through science fiction novels and movies. Why has such virtual/augmented reality become more prevalent in recent years?

It is in the rapid development of technology. Through modern advanced display, network, and sensor technologies, it has become possible to express the virtual world more realistically. Thanks to the advancement of this technology, the general public can now experience the real world of imagination at a reasonable cost. This technology's development has shown endless possibilities for the use of virtual/augmented reality in various industries. New contents are being developed, rushing through this platform as a medium. From now on, let us look at the overall contents of virtual reality and augmented reality as well as the reasons they are rapidly building a new industrial ecosystem.

6.2 What Is Virtual Reality?

First of all, what does virtual reality mean? Virtual reality refers to a technology that induces humans to experience a virtual world built with computers. Virtual reality can be constructed in various ways, and the most widely known method is to attach a head-mounted display to the head and experience virtual reality through a lens. Such scenes will often be seen in virtual reality games or TV programs. In other words, through the lens, the user experiences a three-dimensional simulated environment which incessantly stimulates the human brain, making the user think it is the real environment.

In this case, the user can interact with the surrounding environment through manipulation devices or commands beyond simply immersing in virtual reality. For example, in a virtual reality fighting game, the user becomes the virtual space protagonist and confronts the enemy. Through this, the user becomes more immersed in the game's environment and behaves as if they belong to the environment. Then, what is the difference between augmented reality and virtual reality?

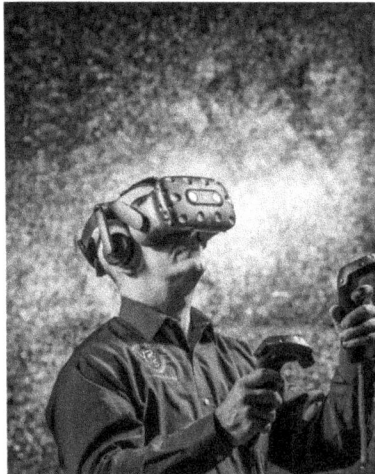

FIGURE 6.1. Virtual reality example (source: "Exploring the Universe in Virtual Reality" by NASA Goddard Photo and Video is licensed under CC BY 2.0).

6.3 Is Augmented Reality Different from Virtual Reality?

Virtual reality builds all the visible environments into a perfect virtual world. Augmented reality is applied by superimposing virtual images on the real environment. This is the most significant difference between virtual reality and augmented reality. Virtual information is augmented based on the real environment and naturally blended into the existing environment. In other words, it is possible to create a synergy effect by adding the advantages of the real world and the virtual world. Then, can we feel the big difference when we experience virtual reality and augmented reality?

Table 6.1. Comparison of Virtual and Augmented Reality

Type	Characteristics
Virtual Reality	• All environments are built in a perfect virtual world.
	• Virtual reality is generally operated through goggles/head-mounted display.
Augmented Reality	• Virtual information is embedded onto a real environment.
	• Augmented reality can be operated through both smartphones and goggles/head-mounted displays.
	• Users can clearly distinguish the real environment and holograms.

For example, suppose we experience a zoo through virtual/augmented reality. In the case of virtual reality, users experience a complete virtual zoo in a three-dimensional space. An imaginary grassland is spread out, and next to it, lively lions and giraffes pass by. Sometimes, things that are impossible in reality are possible, such as a user flying in the sky or swimming in the sea. What would a zoo look like in augmented reality? There is a big difference in using a real environment in an augmented zoo. When the user walks through the real park lawn, he can see a virtual rabbit passing by. Sometimes you can even see a virtual cat hiding through a crack in the school building. In this way, virtual reality and augmented reality present experiences to users in different ways.

The Pokémon Go mobile game, which was once sensational, is also a representative example of applying augmented reality. For example, if you are looking at a specific location with a mobile phone camera, a Pokémon appears on it instantly, and the user tries to catch a Pokémon, and so on. How do we see this virtual/augmented reality space as if it were real?

FIGURE 6.2. Pokémon Go mobile game (source: "pokemon go" by Paintimpact is licensed under CC BY 2.0).

6.4 Do We Believe What We Are Seeing?

It can be said that virtual/augmented reality to date mostly depends on visual devices. So why are we mainly using visual devices? This is because the human brain tends to believe the information it sees easily. For example, when an oasis in the desert appears to be in front of you, such as in a mirage phenomenon, you will believe it is there and continue to pursue it. How about recreating this mirage with modern technology? If you can deceive the human eye by realizing high-resolution displays and 3D spatial information, it can disturb the human brain. More than 70% of the actual human sensory information is related to visual information, and this information enters the optic nerve through the eyes and is transmitted to the brain.

It takes a lot of effort to deceive our eyes and brain completely. In addition to realizing a high-resolution display, objects also need to change quickly when the human gaze moves. When a slight awkward lag occurs, the human brain quickly recognizes it as fake and may trigger a rejection reaction such as motion sickness. Now, the scope of technology is expanding beyond sight to hearing, touch, and smell. When more sensory information is received as real, our brain can be more dazzled. This state is called immersion in the virtual/augmented world. Then, what are the advantages of this virtual/augmented reality for our society?

6.5 What Are the Advantages of Virtual/Augmented Reality?

Virtual/augmented reality has the advantage that we can enjoy various social experiences at a relatively low cost. For example, suppose you want to experience the universe. It requires enormous costs and to be selected as an astronaut. However, if virtual/augmented reality is used, there will be opportunities for many people to experience space at a low cost. In other words, in modern society, virtual/augmented reality is a catalyst that can provide various experiences to people with an excellent cost-performance ratio. At the same time, it can be said to be an indispensable material in the industrial ecosystem.

For this reason, numerous global IT companies are investing heavily in various areas of virtual/augmented reality (hardware, software, content, and platforms). For example, in the case of Google, Magic Leap was acquired for about $2.6 billion, and in the case of Samsung, it started a technical collaboration with Oculus VR. In light of global companies' active investments, the utility and potential value of virtual/augmented reality can be estimated. Then, what kind of virtual/augmented reality equipment is being sold in the current market?

6.6 What Equipment Helps Us Feel Immersed in Virtual Reality?

First, let us look at the equipment that implements virtual reality. Oculus Rift is a virtual reality head-mounted display (HMD) developed by the Oculus VR Company and is one of the most popular products in the market to date. Currently, various options are available, from wireless headset devices to low-cost models. Then, how can it be naturally embodied with environments other than viewing virtual reality through a lens?

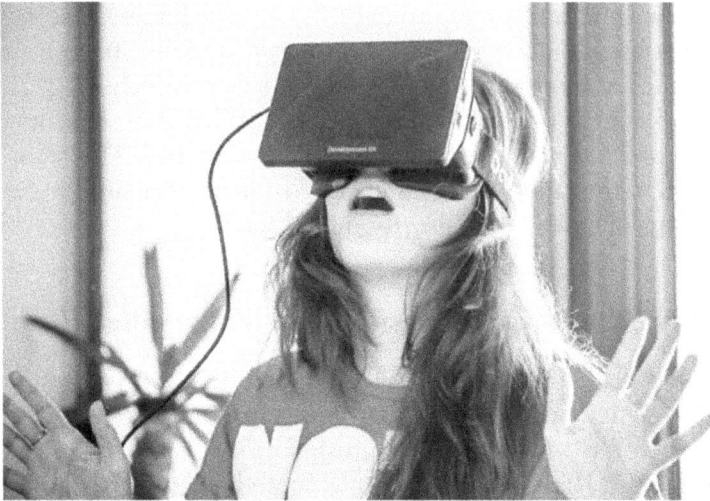

FIGURE 6.3. Example of Oculus Rift (source: "Anna Bashmakova and Oculus Rift" by Sergey Galyonkin is licensed under CC BY-SA 2.0).

For example, suppose we are walking through a fictional city. To feel as if we are in a real city, the surrounding buildings will need to change naturally according to the user's walking pattern. Suppose there is a discrepancy between the user's movement and the environment. In that case, it is difficult for the user to feel immersed in the virtual environment, and side effects such as cyber motion sickness may occur. To compensate for this, a tracking device is built into the headset, and a tracking sensor tracks the location information from the outside. Then, how can the user actively interact with the virtual environment beyond recognizing the user's movement?

Let us go back to the hypothetical city example. When a user opens a door of a building or enters or presses an elevator button, such manipulations and reactions must be made naturally to add a sense of reality. At this time, the user will use the controller. Oculus Touch's controller can be seen as a form that makes the controller of the existing video console game more ergonomic and intuitive. These controllers have a built-in touch sensor to enable complex operation, and a tracking device such as a headset is built-in, allowing natural interaction with the virtual environment. So, are there other products comparable to these headset products?

The Oculus Rift's strong rival, the HTC Vive, cannot be left out. HTC Vive is a virtual reality tangible headset device developed jointly by Valve Corporation and HTC. Like Oculus, this product shows a similar hardware configuration with a headset, controller, and tracking sensor. This product was a latecomer released in 2016 after Oculus, but it quickly dominated the market. One of the reasons is that HTC Vive released exclusive controllers and spatial sensors before Oculus. This technology provided users with a greater sense of immersion and was well received by consumers.

However, the HTC Vive also has relative disadvantages. The HTC Vive is more expensive than the Oculus Rift, requires higher computer specifications, is challenging to install, and requires a long setup time before use. These virtual reality headset devices require high-end computers, and when these costs are combined, it will cost a few thousand dollars. Then, can we not experience virtual reality at a low price?

FIGURE 6.4. HTC Vive (source: "HTC Vive" by wuestenigel is licensed under CC BY 2.0).

As an alternative, there is Google Cardboard, where you can experience virtual reality at a very low cost. How does this work? First, the cardboard is folded based on Google's drawing, and the lens is attached to it. Finally, a simple virtual reality headset is created by inserting a smartphone into the cardboard. In addition to cardboard, Google provides software that can develop virtual reality content. What are the advantages and disadvantages of Google Cardboard compared to the high-end headset devices mentioned previously?

The advantage is that it is at a low price, as expected. Anyone can participate and produce Google Cardboard, and several companies are releasing cardboard with various designs for $10–20. The second advantage is that it is straightforward to use. Google Cardboard is a feature that uses a user's smartphone as a display, and through this, the high resolution and built-in motion sensor of the latest smartphone can be used naturally.

However, there are also disadvantages. The fatal weakness is low operability. It becomes impossible to manipulate the touch screen while using Cardboard. It relies solely on voice recognition and motion sensors. For this reason, there is a regret that the operation is still nonintuitive and the efficiency is low. Another drawback is that there is not much content. Only applications made exclusively for Google Cardboard can be used on smartphones, but the number is small and the quality is often poor. In other words, the machine is provided, but there is not enough content to utilize it, and the tug-of-war between the machine and the content developer has continued for a long time in the virtual reality ecosystem. The machine developer wants to develop different content, but the content developer intends to create high-quality machines that can be used effectively. In the case of Google Cardboard, for now, it seems that the highest application plan is to experience 360-degree videos through platforms such as YouTube. So far, we have looked at various types of virtual reality headset devices. What other devices other than headsets can enhance the user's immersion?

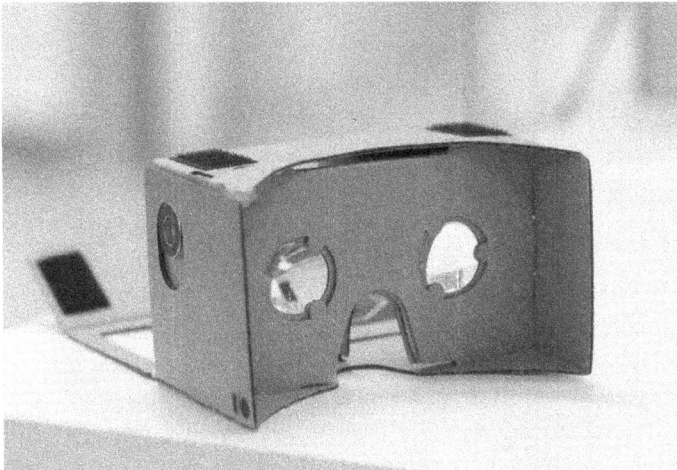

FIGURE 6.5. Google Cardboard (source: "File: Assembled Google Cardboard VR mount. jpg" by othree is licensed under CC BY 2.0).

There is also a virtual reality device in the form of a treadmill that works with the Oculus Rift, as mentioned previously. Allowing users to move freely while experiencing virtual reality is an essential topic in content and equipment development. For example, a device developed by the Virtuix Omni company allows users to walk or run 360 degrees on a treadmill. At this time, the user's safety and functionality are secured by wearing a supporter on the waist and dedicated shoes. In particular, these devices have a significant advantage in recognizing the user's whole-body motions. In contrast, the existing headset only tracks the head's position, and users can experience a more realistic virtual space. In this way, we looked at various equipment that enhances the sense of immersion in virtual reality. Then, what is the equipment that adds a sense of reality in augmented reality?

FIGURE 6.6. Virtuix Omni (source: "Virtuix Omni + Occulus Rift" by Digitas Photos is licensed under CC BY 2.0).

6.7 What Equipment Is Needed for Augmented Reality?

Looking at the equipment of augmented reality, one can think of Microsoft's HoloLens as a representative. HoloLens is a headset-type device and features a fully built-in Windows PC function in the headset body. In other words, we do not need the help of peripheral devices such as a PC or smartphone, and we can think of it as having an independent portable computer on our heads. HoloLens's interaction methods are primarily composed of gaze, gesture, and voice. Users can use their gaze to replace what the mouse has done on the conventional computer.

The user's eyes are recognized by the sensor to naturally switch the screen or select an object only by gaze processing. In the case of gestures, if we follow the posture of the hand designated by HoloLens, we can interact naturally with the environment without pressing a special button. Finally, we can select holograms via voice commands or call up Microsoft's artificial intelligence Cortona. So, how can this HoloLens recognize the real environment and display a hologram that fits it?

The infrared sensor in front of the headset perceives the surrounding space and projects a hologram according to it. For example, we can put an imaginary holographic cat on the sofa in the house as if it were sitting. HoloLens equipped with such advanced functions are expensive products of more than $3,000 and are currently more focused on research and commercial use than the general public. So, was HoloLens the first product to represent augmented reality?

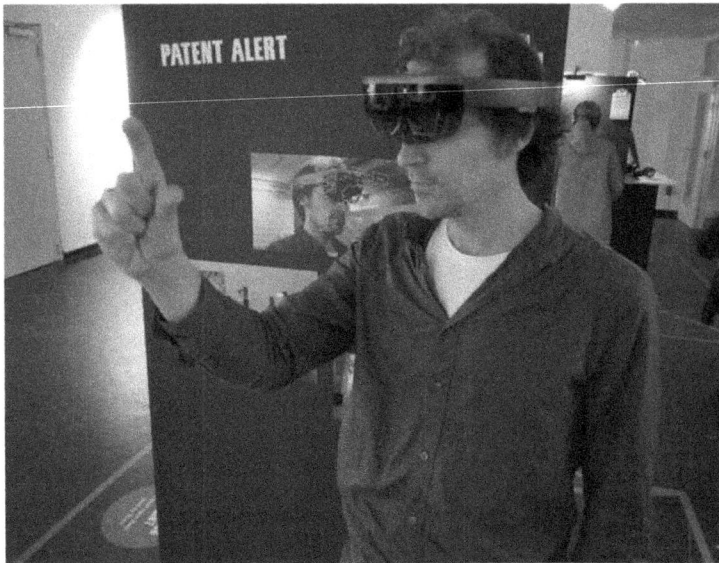

FIGURE 6.7. Microsoft Hololens (source: "Immersive storytelling with Microsoft Hololens device" by sndrv is licensed under CC BY 2.0).

Before releasing Microsoft HoloLens, the first product that caught our attention would have been Google Glass. Google Glass is a headset-type wearable computer, and its developer version was released in 2013. It can be said to be a device similar to the previously mentioned Microsoft HoloLens. Google Glass can record videos or take photos and can perform commands with the voice. Why were these wearable augmented reality products released?

It was to increase user convenience. For example, if we wanted to go to a store and see additional information about the products we wanted in augmented reality, we had to use a smartphone application. However, putting a smartphone on a product like this one by one is cumbersome for busy modern people. To compensate for these shortcomings, wearable smart glasses that can be used naturally were released. These innovative products provoked many topics but unexpectedly failed in the market.

There are many reasons for the failure, but one of the main reasons was that the price was somewhat burdensome for the general public to purchase and that it could invade the general public's privacy. Since it is possible to take photos and videos without others' consent, it could be controversial due to privacy invasion. However, Google is still developing its products steadily and focuses more on applications for specific jobs such as companies, hospitals, and research institutes. How are these virtual/augmented reality devices released to date being practically used in modern society?

FIGURE 6.8. Google Glass (source: "Google Glass" by lawrencegs is licensed under CC BY 2.0).

6.8 Meet Virtual/Augmented Reality in Reality

First, let us look at a business application case of virtual reality. The unique sense of concentration and immersion that virtual reality evokes is already in the spotlight in entertainment fields such as games and movies. The medium of games has a significant advantage in allowing users to learn how to use devices naturally while feeling pleasure. In particular, new devices and platforms such as virtual reality can cause users to feel rejection at an early stage, which is naturally habituated through the medium of games. For example, a game called "Bit Saver" surpassed 1 million copies for the first time in a virtual reality game. This game allows us to cut blocks and avoid obstacles according to the rhythm of the music, and users have highly praised it for its spectacular performance.

In social science and psychology, virtual reality can be a cost-effective experimental device that can set an experiment environment and interaction. Virtual reality can also be used as therapy to relieve anxiety symptoms. For example, to treat soldiers suffering from post-traumatic stress syndrome (PTSD) after the war, a virtual battle scene is reproduced step by step, and the symptoms can be alleviated when combined with a doctor's counseling. Virtual reality is also used in rehabilitation to diagnose older adults with Alzheimer's disease. For example, one could find patients with potential high risk of developing dementia while having patients find their way in a virtual space. In medical surgery, virtual reality is also used as an inexpensive and effective surgical training method. There is an educational advantage, because we can experience various surgical sites and procedures without directly entering the operating room.

Virtual reality can also be used in general education. Using virtual reality, existing educational materials can be used to enhance educational effects through audio-visual stimulation, and the past world that exists only in history can be experienced virtually more clearly. Virtual reality can also be applied to the tourism industry. By allowing customers to virtually experience travel destinations they have not been to, more intuitive travel destination selection is possible, and background knowledge of travel destinations can also be naturally acquired.

A world in which artistic expression is also possible through virtual reality has arrived. For example, if we use a virtual reality app called Tilt Brush, we can freely move and draw in a three-dimensional virtual space. With the advantage of such a space that is not limited, creative works can be drawn, and viewers can directly enter the virtual space and appreciate the work in a three-dimensional sense. Then, what business application examples exist in the case of augmented reality?

FIGURE 6.9. Tilt Brush (source: "Tilt Brush de Google (Salon Viva Technology, Paris)" by dalbera is licensed under CC BY 2.0).

Augmented reality also has excellent commercial potential and is already being actively applied in many fields. For example, Google uses an augmented reality navigation function with Google Maps to help users quickly and easily find directions by showing arrows and direction indicators on the camera view when wandering in the street. Augmented reality is already in the spotlight in e-commerce and is developing at a rapid pace. For example, furniture sold in stores can be placed virtually all over the house through mobile phone cameras, enabling more rational decision-making. Already, IKEA and many domestic and foreign furniture and interior companies have begun offering this service. Clothes sold in Internet shopping malls can also be worn virtually on consumers' actual appearance, helping more rational shopping.

The sports industry is also starting to adopt augmented reality. For example, in broadcasting a billiard game, the moment a player prepares to hit the ball, the expected trajectory is drawn on the pool table. This not only helps viewers understand but can also strengthen the entertainment side. Recently, a culture of enjoying games simultaneously with climbing has emerged by grafting augmented reality onto indoor climbing walls. Augmented reality is being actively applied to education fields such as anatomy, and infinite development is expected in the future.

6.9 Problems to Be Solved in Virtual/Augmented Reality

Virtual reality and augmented reality have many advantages and potentials, but side effects are problematic due to the introduction of new technologies. First, in the case of virtual reality, there are concerns about health and safety. While immersed in virtual reality, we may trip over an actual obstacle or be shocked by an object, or we may feel uncomfortable in our neck, shoulders, or back if we use it for a long time. Some users have seizure symptoms or faint with the use of virtual reality. Besides, using a virtual reality headset for a long time can cause eyestrain. Research shows that when a person is looking at the screen, they blink less, and they tend to have a drier eye than when they do not. There is also a symptom called virtual reality cybersickness. It is similar to the symptoms of motion sickness that we experience when we board a boat or car, and it causes headaches, abdominal pain, nausea, vomiting, fatigue, drowsiness, and dizziness. So, what are some of the concerns in augmented reality?

In the case of augmented reality, it can lead to dangers in real environments. According to a recent paper published by Purdue University in the United States, a significant number of vehicle accidents, injuries, and deaths occurred due to the Pokémon Go game's use while driving.[1] Due to the immersion of augmented reality, the user may become numb to the dangers of the surrounding environment. Besides, invasion of privacy cannot be ignored. The other party's personal information can be easily exposed to the user through face recognition of the augmented reality device. This information can be disclosed to the other person regardless of intention by linking with social media and other media. Legal and ethical measures are being taken against such privacy infringement.

---

[1] *Faccio, Mara, and John J. McConnell. 2020. "Death by Pokémon GO: The economic and human cost of using apps while driving." Journal of Risk and Insurance 87, no. 3: 815–849.*

FIGURE 6.10. Warning message of the Pokémon Go (source: "Pokémon Go!" by IainStars is licensed under CC BY-SA 2.0).

6.10 Virtual/Augmented Reality, What Is the Future Direction

What kind of effort is needed to further revitalize the virtual/augmented reality industry in the future? Recently, a new concept of Mixed Reality or Extended Reality, which combines the advantages of virtual reality and augmented reality, has emerged. For example, in the movie *Kingsman: The Golden Circle*, there is a scene where secret agents wear special glasses and virtually gather together in an office in London for a meeting. Due to the realization of three-dimensional graphics in this scene, agents naturally feel and interact as if other agents were next to them. Is this mixed reality possible? For this purpose, technical limitations such as processing large-capacity data still exist. Furthermore, in recent years, attempts have been made to stimulate the user's five senses further and enhance immersion by introducing audiovisual information of the user and smell and tactile information. Like a hologram using a drone as shown in *Spider-Man: Far from Home*, in the near future, the real and virtual worlds will melt so naturally that we may not be able to distinguish them, and new ethics and regulations will arise accordingly.

Many experts predict that the market of virtual reality and augmented reality will grow in earnest from now on. In virtual reality, development is currently being made around the machine itself. Still, it is expected that the role of a platform that provides content will be more emphasized in the future. As many companies, from global companies to startups, apply virtual reality and commercialize products accordingly, rapid growth is expected in the future. The business is currently mainly focused on games and entertainment content, but it is expected to expand to various fields such as medical care, shopping, and advertisement in the future. Now, technology development is shifting from the current hardware development of virtual reality to software content. It is expected that competition in applied software technology will be an essential factor in the future. So, what is the prospect of augmented reality?

In the case of augmented reality, like virtual reality, it is overgrowing. Until now, due to technical limitations, it can be said that augmented reality headsets were more like little clunky goggles than natural wearable glasses. In the future, it is expected that smaller types of devices will be released due to technological advances. For example, the American start-up Mojo Vision has unveiled a built-in smart contact lens. Through this lens, virtual information can be combined with the real environment.

Some are also forecasting that the augmented reality market may be several times larger than that of virtual reality. So, what is the reason? Unlike virtual reality, augmented reality has a strong point in content development efficiency in that it does not have to create all environments. In other words, there are endless areas that can be utilized depending on how the existing reality background and hologram are combined. Augmented reality is expected to grow significantly in fields such as the e-commerce and advertising industries. These features show characteristics similar to the business growth of early smartphones. The initial smartphone devices and services did not bring much appeal, but as various attempts were made to use them as a platform, the market accelerated and grew explosively. It seems that virtual/augmented reality could follow this trend.

6.11 What if the Distinction between Reality and Virtual Disappears?

Tesla founder Elon Musk once said, "The probability of future human beings living in real reality, not in a virtual world, is only one in one billion."

Like the movie *The Matrix*, even if we do not wear a headset, there may be an era in which all human nervous systems share the same virtual reality by accessing the body's input terminals. Given the exponential growth of technology against Moore's Law[2], these things may not be impossible. What will happen to humankind when the real and virtual worlds are put in a world where the world becomes unclear? It is difficult to give a clear answer as to whether this will be poison to humankind or an opportunity to advance to a better world. The essence of virtual/augmented reality is a technology that turns imagination into reality and sometimes reality into imagination. When these technologies reach their peak in the distant future, we look forward to seeing what the world will look like.

---

[2] *Schaller, Robert R. 1997. "Moore's law: past, present and future." IEEE spectrum 34, no. 6: 52–59.*

7

BLOCKCHAIN

7.1 Why Blockchain?

Since the introduction of cryptocurrency to the public, there has been a frenzy of cryptocurrency investment, led by Bitcoin. Numerous people jumped into a new concept of an investment product called cryptocurrency and were enthusiastic about it. In the media, the news that cryptocurrency has made tremendous profits has attracted people's attention. People were interested in a new type of investment asset but relatively lacked interest in the technology that made it possible. The core technology of cryptocurrency is blockchain.[1] The cryptocurrency was just one example of the application of blockchain technology, but many people only focus on Bitcoin rather than on blockchain, the core technology. However, blockchain itself is one of the core technologies in the era of the 4th Industrial Revolution. Besides, global IT companies have already designated blockchain as a core technology and are applying and developing it in various application fields. So, let us look first at what a blockchain is.

It is necessary to understand the current financial system's payment and settlement system[2] to understand blockchain. The payment and settlement process of funds that supports real economic activities and financial transactions occurs in an ecosystem called the financial system. In other words,

---

[1] *For example, South Korea's government announced on June 30, 2020, the policy to develop core source technologies, aiming to intensively foster blockchain and technologies such as artificial intelligence, the IoT, and cloud computing.*

[2] *It refers to a procedure for transferring funds between bonds and debt relationships between the parties to a transaction when a transaction occurs while economic actors engage in economic activities. You can think of cash, checks, drafts, credit cards, bank transfers, etc., that individuals use.*

(a) financial institutions, (b) financial markets, and (c) financial products or services corresponding to the movement of funds are the main components of this ecosystem. For example, currency supports the economic activities of firms/households through financial institutions. Moreover, households generate income through labor, and the surplus remaining after consumption is transferred to financial institutions in the form of savings. These savings continue to circulate within the economic system through the intermediary function[3] of a financial institution. Most economic transactions involve the movement of funds between entities participating in the transaction. For example, when purchasing a product with a credit card, funds are transferred from the credit card company's bank account to the affiliated store (where the product is purchased), and legally protected debt contracts are established between the credit card company and the credit card user. On the payment date of the credit card, the debt contract is extinguished by the transfer of funds from the account of the credit card user to the account of the credit card firm. In addition, if funds are insufficient to purchase a house, the household can borrow funds in the form of a mortgage loan. As shown in the previous example, money transfer in everyday economic life is carried out through financial firms. Representative entities in the current financial system are as follows:

- Central Bank

- Financial Institutions (e.g., banks)

- Households, Firms, Government

A central bank issues fiat money, and it manages the amount of money in the economic system. Banks and financial firms receive funds from customers in deposits and provide funds to those in need. Moreover, banks play a vital role in the movement of all funds involved in the economic activities of households, companies, and governments described previously. In other words, banks (financial firms) and a central bank are crucial elements in the transfer of funds between economic entities, which is the basis of all economic activity transactions.

For example, in the United States, money transfers between banks are done by the Fedwire (formerly known as Federal Reserve Wire Network). The transaction of securities (e.g., stocks, bonds) is carried out by the

---

[3] *Funds are supplied to subjects in need of money so that economic activities can take place smoothly. Money is collected from subjects with extra funds and delivered to those in need. Financial institutions are primarily responsible for the transfer of funds through loans, bonds, stocks, and credit cards.*

Depository Trust & Clearing Corporation (DTCC). The key point here is the fact that in the current financial system, the transfer of funds and settlement process is centralized by financial firms or state federal payment/settlement institutions. In other words, banks check and manage the validity of all routine money transactions (transfers) and record them in their database systems.[4] Therefore, financial companies are responsible for verifying the validity of a particular transaction, and financial institutions are also responsible for managing records of that transaction.[5]

Under the current financial system, to carry out daily electronic money transfers, there is no choice but to go through a financial firm. Such a centralized payment and settlement system has advantages, but there are inefficiencies such as delays, security vulnerabilities, and transaction fees.[6]

The records of money transactions between banks are recorded and managed by the central bank, the entity with centralized authority. For example, suppose you remit a thousand dollars to a friend by Internet banking; a financial intermediary such as a bank creates and manages records of these new transactions. When you are sending money to a friend who has an account with the same bank, the bank is just changing the record (ledger) that exists on the server.[7] In other words, deducting a thousand dollars from the balance of the sender's account and increasing the recipient's account balance by a thousand dollars is the core of a series of the fund transfer process. The transfer of funds between other banks is also not significantly different: deducting the balance from the remittance bank account through the payment and settlement system and increasing the balance in the receiving bank account causes the transfer of funds, of course, incurs a fee, and overseas remittances go through a similar process.[8] In other words, the task of handling the movement of funds between economic entities in the current financial system is

---

[4] *Except for cash transactions, all transactions are managed by an account (ledger) on the bank's computer server.*

[5] *Only the financial company that keeps all the transaction details can verify whether the transaction details are accurate and that nothing is missing.*

[6] *It takes at least a day or more to transfer dollars from Korea to the United States. So, there's a joke that the fastest way to do it is to load it on an airplane (of course, there are shipping charges).*

[7] *Remittance is made by adjusting the number of books on the computer without the process of actual cash movement.*

[8] *Even if funds are transferred from Korea to the United States by exchange of money, money transfer between countries is not actually performed, and the amount of the transfer is deducted from the account in Korea and the amount in the account held by the Korean bank in the United States bank is transferred to the customer.*

nothing more than managing a vast database. However, only financial companies and related authorized institutions are responsible for the management. The key feature of this transfer system is that the responsibility and authority to check the validity of transactions and prevent manipulation of transaction records are only awarded to financial companies and a few related institutions. Let us learn more about the ledger in the following.

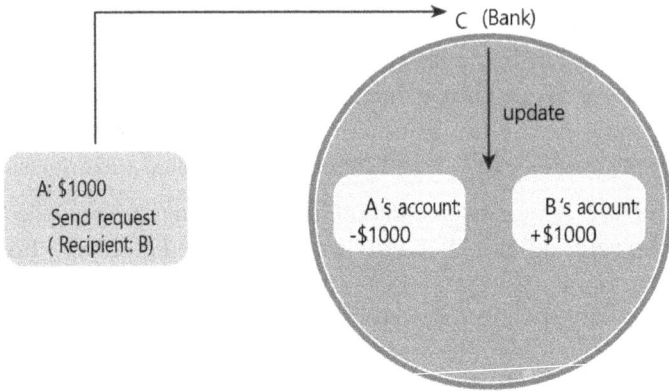

FIGURE 7.1. Money transfer in the current financial system (transfer within the same bank).

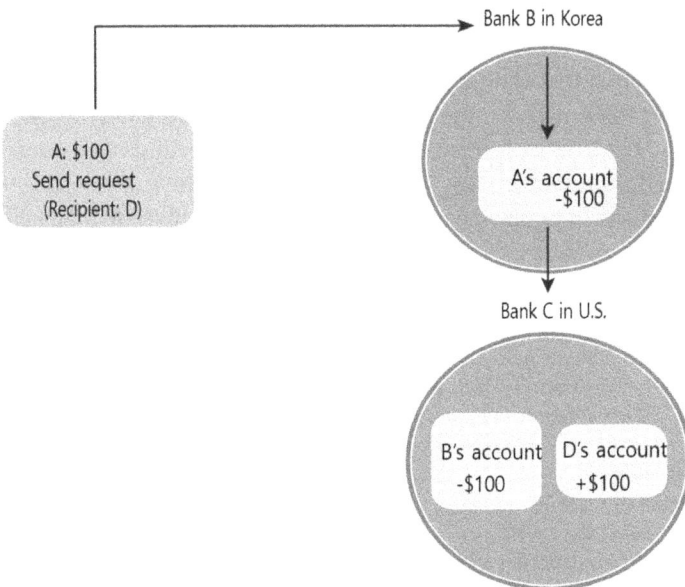

FIGURE 7.2. Cross-border money transfer in the current financial system.

7.2 What Is a Ledger?

To understand the blockchain[9], the concept of a ledger must be understood first. A ledger is a book that records and transacts all transactions. The pocket money register that we used as a child and the household account book that homemakers write is also a ledger. The ledger is a kind of book that contains the details of the transactions in which money flows. It is easy to think that the ledger is a household account book if you write it at home and an account book if you write it at a company.

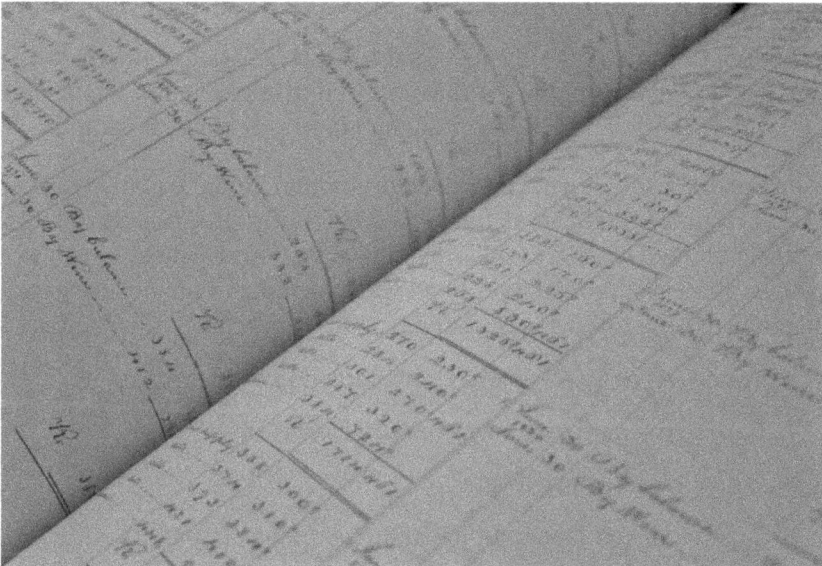

FIGURE 7.3. Traditional ledger (source: "Accounts book" by futureshape is licensed under CC BY 2.0).

Let's imagine how the flow of the funds is being created through the ledger. Suppose Mike lends $1 to Jane. It will be easy to think about how it is written in each other's pocket money register. The transfer of $1 from Mike to Jane will be a transaction, and the participants in the transaction will be Mike and Jane. For the transaction to take place, either directly forwarding $1 or sending it through internet banking, this transaction is fulfilled. Though this is an extreme example, we do not see any problem in this type of transaction because there are countless examples of these types

---

[9] *Blockchain can be referred to as "distributed ledger technology," but we will cover more details later.*

of transactions in our lives. However, in fact, there are many inefficiencies in this type of transaction. Consider what inefficiencies exist.

- First and foremost, banks may charge a fee for transferring money through internet banking. There was a cost for the transaction.[10]

- Mike lent his $1 to Jane. Mike entered the transaction in his pocket money entry ($1 was reduced from his pocket) and Jane in her pocket money entry ($1 increased). Instead of recording that she increased $1 in her pocket money entry, she just spent 100 won elsewhere. And to Mike, she can argue that she never borrowed money from him.

- Suppose that Mike has decided to lend his $1 to Jane. But he only has foreign currency. In that case, he must exchange money. When Internet banking is not working, he must meet and give it to her.

Although the case above is an extreme situation, in the payment and settlement system of the current financial system, the previous inconvenience, inefficiency, and weakness in verifying transactions exist. As a result, many people who have noticed a problem with the current financial system have begun to ask the following questions:

- Can we store assets (money) with trust forever?

- Can we track who manages financial assets (money)?

- Can we easily move assets?

- Can we make a transaction without costs (fees)?

Although many people have had the previous problems for a long time, the existing solid financial system has remained unchanged for a long time. There may be various reasons for this, but nothing else could replace the existing financial system. Furthermore, it was not easy to solve the previous problem due to various complex interests among the various entities in the existing system.[11] However, attempts to break the existing rules and build a new system began to materialize, and in this process, the blockchain came into the world.

---

[10] *It is usually free, but if there is a fee, it's a bigger deal than expected.*

[11] *Even in areas where innovation is possible, various interests are often intertwined, so it is always difficult to break the existing order and build a new system.*

7.3 Emergence of Blockchain: Bitcoin

Satoshi Nakamoto[12] is known to have provided the first idea of the blockchain. Many people claimed that he was Satoshi, and it is not clear where he lived or his origin. He was the creator of the first cryptocurrency, Bitcoin.[13]

Satoshi Nakamoto created Bitcoins using blockchain technology, and since he first started mining in early 2009, it is estimated that there are about 1 million Bitcoins in his wallet.[14] Satoshi seems to have been aware of the problems with the existing centralized financial system. For example, Satoshi Nakamoto posted the following thoughts on the current financial system:

> Confidence is essential that the traditional currency will not devalue the central bank. However, in the history of legal currency, this belief has often been abandoned. For example, the 2008 U.S. subprime mortgage crisis is a prime example. As long as their credit rating is poor, they have provided mortgage loans to people who cannot afford to pay them back. At that time, the interest rate was low even when receiving a mortgage loan because it was a low-interest rate, and house prices were steadily rising due to an increase in demand for the house. From the bank's point of view, the house's price continued to rise, and even if the borrower could not repay it, it was an advantage because it was possible to obtain a house held as collateral. However, demand declined due to too high real estate prices, and loan interest increased due to an interest rate hike. As the subprime class fell into default, and the property increased, the house price collapsed.

---

[12] *It is not confirmed whether he is a real person, and as the name suggests, many assume that he is Japanese, but this has not been confirmed.*

[13] *Bitcoin and blockchain are sometimes used interchangeably, but they do not mean the same thing. Blockchain refers to a data distribution processing technology called a "public transaction ledger," and Bitcoin is a type of cryptocurrency developed by applying blockchain.*

[14] *Satoshi is the founder of Bitcoin and is estimated to own about $15 billion of Bitcoin as of June 2019. Based on the value of Bitcoin, a cryptocurrency, he is the world's 100th richest person.*

FIGURE 7.4. Satoshi Nakamoto, Bitcoin founder (source: "Satoshi Nakamoto Bitcoin Founder" by BeatingBetting is licensed under CC BY 2.0).

As a result, the criticism of the existing centralized financial system was very intense, and it seems that at that time, Satoshi Nakamoto wanted to create a new type of financial system, which is less vulnerable to cybersecurity risk, that could continue to operate without financial intermediaries. Satoshi Nakamoto published a 9-page paper on November 1, 2008, which proposed a new money transfer system entitled "Bitcoin: A Peer-to-Peer Electronic Cash System."[15]

Based on the seminal paper, in 2009, he developed the world's first cryptocurrency, Bitcoin, which is the first blockchain management program (Bitcoin Core) proposed and implemented by Satoshi Nakamoto. He distributed the address of the site where he uploaded his thesis to cryptography experts by email.[16]

This 9-page paper explains the basic structure of the first blockchain and Bitcoin, but it is not easy for the public to understand due to the technical content of the paper. However, the key is to propose a technology concept of blockchain and use the technology to introduce Bitcoin as one of its applications. The first blockchain management program—Bitcoin Core— was designed to create bitcoin, a cryptocurrency, and record Bitcoin transactions in the form of a blockchain. To verify the records of the blockchain,

---

[15] *The original text is available at https://bitcoin.org/bitcoin.pd.*

[16] *In the email, a new concept of P2P electronic money system was introduced, along with a link to the Bitcoin white paper.*

it is necessary to participate in the blockchain system network, and by participating in this, Bitcoin is provided as a reward for participating in the blockchain verification process. He developed Bitcoin, the first cryptocurrency to which blockchain technology was applied, and distributed the written source code. In the process, he solved the double-payment problem[17] for a digital currency for the first time using the Peer-to-Peer network.

The Bitcoin system is designed to make it progressively more difficult to generate the next Bitcoin each time a new Bitcoin is created through Bitcoin, software, and distributed networks. Bitcoin, which used to be mined for hours on individual computers, can now only be obtained by running for weeks or months on thousands of specialized mining computers.[18]

FIGURE 7.5. Bitcoin mining factory (source: "Bitcoin mining" by Marko is licensed under CC BY 2.0).

Satoshi Nakamoto tried to create a decentralized system that allows individuals to directly transact away from the existing centralized financial system (the way governments or banks facilitate financial transactions) using blockchain technology. Nobody can cast doubt on the claim that he played a significant role in creating, introducing, and popularizing a new concept of a cryptocurrency called Bitcoin.

---

[17] *The double-spending problem will be covered later in the book.*

[18] *So, to mine Bitcoins, there are specialized mining sites using a huge number of PCs in regions where electricity is low in China, and the price of GPU, a core component for mining, has skyrocketed. The amount of electricity consumed for bitcoin mining has been so large that we are now measuring the amount of electricity consumed to generate Bitcoins relative to the total electricity consumption.*

7.4 Double-Spending Problem

Bitcoin attempted to make financial transactions between individuals efficiently and without going through the current financial system.[19] Among the issues that can arise in a decentralized money transfer system is something called "double-spending." Literally, it is a problem that occurs when payments are made twice (double) with the same currency.

When using a bank under the current financial system, each bank has a central control system, so if you proceed in the order in which the transaction requests are made, double-spending can't occur. For example, if A requests to transfer $1,000 to B and C simultaneously (when A's balance is $1,000), the central system processes the transaction requests sequentially. If the remittance request comes into B first, the transaction is processed first in the order, and the amount is deducted. In the case of a remittance request to C, the balance of A has already reached 0, so you can print out an insufficient balance error. If the bank remits $1,000 to B, the balance will be 0, so it will not be possible to send $1,000 to C. The double-spending problem is not arising because the bank manages the transaction data in a centralized manner. If the transaction details are not recorded in the centralized ledger, $1,000 may be transferred to B and C even if the balance is insufficient at the request of A, which is called the double-spending problem.

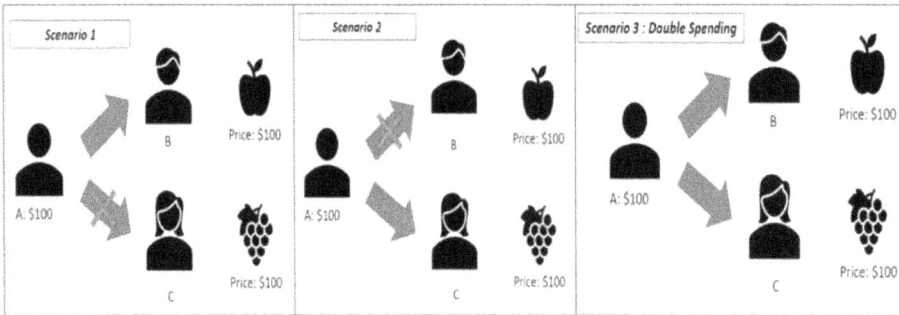

FIGURE 7.6. Examples of double-spending: In the real world or in a centralized financial system, a person with $100 can only pay $100 (scenario 1, scenario 2). However, in the decentralized system, even if a person with $100 has insufficient balance, double payment can occur in which money can be remitted to several people.

---

[19] *Bitcoin aims to execute the transfer of funds between individuals without intermediaries such as banks.*

Suppose there is no central organization with authority such as banks. How did the new financial system that Bitcoin wanted to implement solve the double payment problem? The Bitcoin network solved the double payment problem by using the consensus algorithm as proof of work.

In simple terms, the consensus algorithm is that every time a bitcoin transaction is made, all network participants confirm (verify) and agree on the transaction details. Since all transaction details must be shared and verified by network participants, the transaction details are kept separately. In this way, all participants in the network verify and agree on transaction details.[20] In this process, the network participant's computing power is required to solve complex problems, and cryptocurrency (Bitcoin) is rewarded to participants for providing computing power to the verification process.[21]

7.5 What Is a Blockchain?

Blockchain is a distributed ledger shared data storage technology implemented on a transaction network. The ledger described previously finally appears here. In the centralized financial system so far, all ledgers are not distributed and stored but are recorded and stored in a specific institution. For example, the information we deposit/transmit/withdraw from a bank is stored in the ledger system managed by the bank. In the past, all these transactions were recorded on a paper ledger, but now they are recorded on a computer system. With the current technology and system, financial transactions in our society are impossible now without a ledger (book) record created by a trustworthy central institution.[22] Blockchain can escape the reality of relying on such a centralized ledger and solve the problems (inefficiency, cost, etc.) of the current financial system.

7.6 How Does Blockchain Work?

A blockchain is literally a set of blocks connected by a chain. A block is a kind of data storage space, and you can think of as there is a ledger that contains various transaction information in the block. Participants

---

[20] *This is the process performed by the blockchain management program.*
[21] *This process can be understood as mining.*
[22] *In addition to the double-spending problem described previously, how can we prove and verify that money is exchanged when transacting with each other if each has different books and only has their own information? There will be unimaginable confusion.*

who participate in the blockchain network have blocks on their PCs, and the blocks are all connected like a chain, and this connected blockchain becomes a ledger. If even a single piece of information is changed, the changed information is copied/shared to all participants, and all the originals are recorded, stored, transmitted, and synchronized. Since all blocks are connected by a chain called a hash (a code that encrypts the records of transactions in the block and the hash code of the previous block), money transfers are executed in this connected and shared environment. Because information is shared, the blockchain is called a distributed ledger shared data storage technology.

Since all transaction details are shared and stored on a computer in the blockchain network, even if a specific individual or a few participants intentionally change the information, it is filtered through the verification algorithm, making it impossible to change or manipulate. Furthermore, peer-to-peer transactions are also possible. Since there are no intermediaries involved, there is no commission. Since cryptocurrency is exchanged online, it is possible to trade without restrictions in time and space. Whenever a transaction is made, the details of the transaction are verified through the verification process of the blockchain participants, and it is technically and theoretically impossible to manipulate the ledger or forge financial transactions.

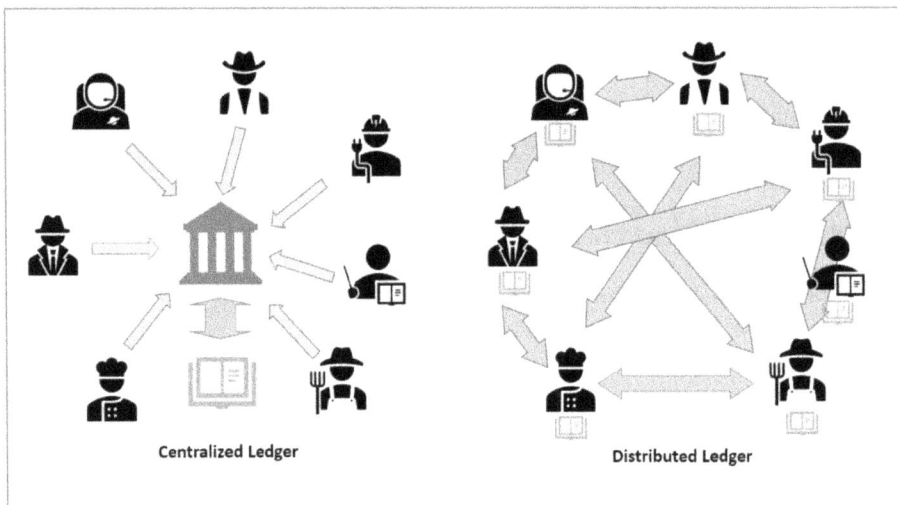

Centralized Ledger   Distributed Ledger

FIGURE 7.7. Centralized ledger versus decentralized ledger.

7.7 How Does Cryptocurrency Work?

Let's see a little more about how cryptocurrency (including Bitcoin) is exchanged. All transactions made within the blockchain network are recorded and stored in a block. Even if only one transaction is made, the timestamp of the transaction and data information is recorded in a continuous chain. The details of transactions stored in this way are encrypted and protected through the blockchain, and all transactions are recorded (digital log files). Each time this transaction is made, new information is continuously added and stored in the chain, and after network participants verify and agree on this transaction through the mining process, the transaction is concluded. And then the cryptocurrency is delivered.[23]

In this way, P2P (Peer-to-Peer) transactions can be made purely using cryptocurrency without going through financial institutions as in traditional financial transactions. The double-spending problem described previously is also prevented through verification and agreement of participants. Since Bitcoin's blockchain publicly distributes and shares all ledgers (transaction ledgers), each participant can check all transactions in the blockchain (in an encrypted state).

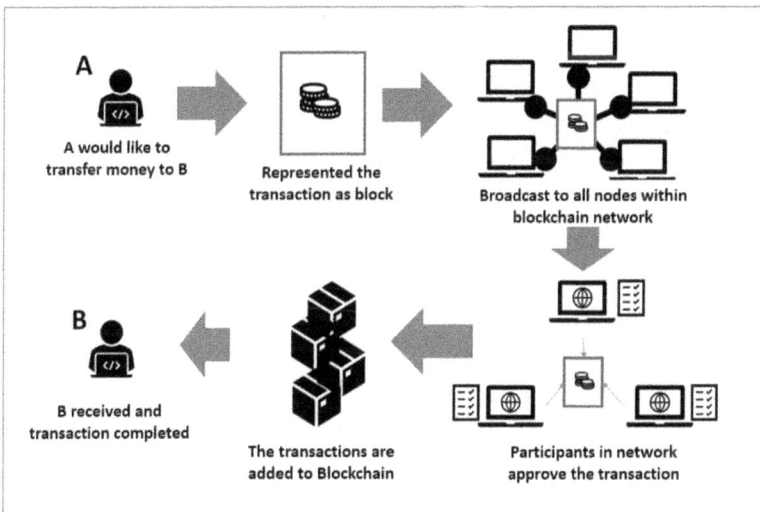

FIGURE 7.8. Process of exchange of cryptocurrency.

---

[23] *When it is said that Bitcoins are transferred from A to B, the transfer is completed after verification and agreement.*

7.8 Why Is Blockchain Good?

In this section, we will look at the benefits of blockchain technology:

1) **Blockchain guarantees the validity and integrity of transactions.**

   One of the most important factors in a transaction is trust. Many transactions between various parties are based on trust. For example, suppose you need to confirm the country of origin when you go to the market and buy beef. When you want to know if this meat is from the U.S., Korea, or Australia, we look at the country-of-origin information provided by the butcher. The unpleasant aspect of this case is that the information on beef has no choice but to be trusted. How many times do people eat beef without knowing that it is imported? It is a sad reality that you are probably deceived without knowing it. That is why we buy products of the same quality more expensively at more expensive but more reliable stores. This behavior starts with the premise that some stores are more reliable. To avoid being deceived and not being scammed, you pay more. If the beef product has a barcode and, scanning it with the camera of my smartphone, the origin of the beef, the distribution process, and the history of the movement of the product are revealed, the reliability will increase. As such, there is no reason not to change it in such a way if the data of all transactions produced, moved, and sold by the beef product are valid and intact. This suggests the possibility that blockchain can bring innovation to the food material distribution system. We will explain more with examples later, but it can be said that blockchain is the technology that will lead the innovation of the existing way of life and business by applying blockchain technology across our society and industries.

2) **It is possible to conduct personal-to-individual transactions in a reliable environment without delay and cost caused by third parties or intermediaries.**

   We use intermediaries (also called agents) in many areas in which we live and for many of the transactions being made. In addition to standardized products, when value fluctuates or product information is insufficient, a broker is often used. Examples of brokers around us are as follows.

   • Real estate broker when renting or purchasing an apartment

   • Cross-border money transfer: foreign remittance

- When purchasing agricultural and marine products through a market merchant rather than through direct transactions

Although it is difficult to define the role of an intermediary simply, it can be said that in addition to facilitating transactions—in the case of real estate, the role of finding and introducing properties—it can also act as a safety plate for risk management in the transaction process. Intermediaries sometimes can manage various risks that may occur in direct transactions between individuals, or they can play a role in reducing risk factors that may occur in financial transactions. Clients using these intermediary services are paying fees in return. Also, various documents required in signing a contract, along with the cost incurred, and the time required are costs, which is a kind of inefficiency. Blockchain can lay the foundation for direct peer-to-peer (person-to-person) transactions without such intermediaries and related costs.

For example, suppose you remit dollars from South Korea to another country. This cross-border money transaction will take at least one or two business days. The current global financial system is a structure in which several banks located across the globe act as intermediaries, and they receive commissions in return for facilitating cross-border money transactions. However, if you use a cryptocurrency implemented in a blockchain, you can send it from one wallet to other wallets in a few minutes with very low costs compared to fees imposed by traditional intermediaries.[24] Geographical location does not matter.

3) **Blockchain is an opportunity for innovation for businesses.**

Through the various advantages of blockchain technology (i.e., effectiveness, integrity, efficiency, low cost), companies can have endless applications across the industry. That is why many global companies are participating in and developing the blockchain market. Cryptocurrency is only one application field. It is a technology that can be applied to many different industries, including finance, the public sector, healthcare, and logistics. We will discuss the applications of blockchain technology in detail in the last section of this chapter.

---

[24] *Bitcoin is not transmitted in real time due to technical factors. This is because it takes some time to verify the transaction. However, in the case of other cryptocurrencies, real-time transmission is technically possible.*

7.9 Types of Blockchain

The type of blockchain is determined by the form of the participants participating in the blockchain network. In other words, it is classified according to the eligibility to participate in the blockchain network. Blockchains can be divided into three types:

1. A public blockchain: open type
2. Private blockchain: closed type
3. Hybrid blockchain: a mixed type of public and private

1. *Public Blockchain*

A public blockchain is said to be an open blockchain in which anyone can freely participate. Anyone can join the blockchain network in any environment where the Internet is connected. It is called a public (open) blockchain because anyone who wants to participate in a specific blockchain network can participate using devices (computers, smartphones, servers, computer miners) connected to the network (Internet). Since the subject of operation and participation is unclear, to induce participation, tokens, which are an incentive system, that is, cryptocurrencies, such as Bitcoin, are issued. Individual devices participating in the blockchain are called nodes. Each node can copy/store information stored in the blockchain and perform operations (for verification of transactions) to create new blocks. Cryptocurrencies such as Bitcoin and Ethereum are operated as open-type blockchains. Therefore, anyone can participate in the blockchain network to trade and mine bitcoins.

2. *Private Blockchain*

A private blockchain is a blockchain network created with a specific purpose by a particular organization. Therefore, it is a blockchain that does not allow anyone to participate in the blockchain network. Only those who have permission from an organization can participate in the blockchain network. Since the subject of operation and participation is clear, there is no need to issue coins such as cryptocurrency to induce participation. Since the administrator of an institution or company is predetermined and managed by a specific entity, participants (nodes) must get permission from the administrator to access the blockchain, data management and verification, and transaction details. Many private blockchains are being introduced to centrally control the system and take, at the same time, various advantages of blockchain under a system currently operating in a distributed database. Wal-Mart, a large retailer in the United States, has developed a system that can check hygiene conditions in real time by applying private blockchain technology to the entire production and distribution process of food ingredients. Given that, in the United States, most fresh ingredients are imported from Mexico and South America, Wal-Mart tracks the entire logistic process of such ingredients using private blockchain technology. In addition, Samsung SDS developed a used car history management system by applying blockchain technology, which is also an example of a private blockchain. The used car market is a good example of applying blockchain.[25] Used car buyers are bound to be sensitive to the accident history of the vehicle. In such a private blockchain, a vehicle's repair and accident history cannot be counterfeited or altered.

3. Hybrid Blockchain

Hybrid blockchain is a mixture of public and private blockchains. Since it is a blockchain that combines the advantages of both and can complement the shortcomings of the existing form and maximize the benefits, it is expected to spread rapidly in the future.[26]

Table 7.1. Type of Blockchain

Type	Degree of Openness	Degree of Decentralization
Public Blockchain	High	High
Private Blockchain	Low	Low
Hybrid Blockchain	Middle	Middle

---

[25] *Due to the nature of the used car market, there are many dealers or intermediaries, and for this reason, it is a good field in which to apply blockchain.*

[26] *Hybrid blockchain is a technology that connects public and private blockchains or has both features. Although it sacrifices a bit of decentralization, which is the philosophy of the blockchain, it is possible to focus on convenience and service from the user's point of view by increasing the convenience of management.*

7.10 Business Applications of Blockchain

In this section, we will look at business applications and use cases using blockchain technology:

1. *Finance*

   The financial sector, including banking, is a representative sector that operates conservatively and traditionally. With the development of IT technology, accessibility to financial services is higher than in the past, and financial services can be used more conveniently, but looking carefully it is only the extent to which the existing work method was made more efficient by using IT technology. For example, in the past, when you wanted to open an account or get a loan at a bank, you visited the bank to apply for and use a document-based application. Although the service can be accessed via Internet banking, the work process has not changed significantly. Due to the nature of dealing with money, finance's work requires a high level of accuracy. Besides, the degree of human involvement in the work process is high. There is a limit to the innovation of the industry itself due to the inefficiency of the existing payment system, limited transparency, and security weaknesses.

   Blockchain technology can solve the current financial industry limitations through a responsible and transparent governance system, improved consensus among stakeholders, faster processing of business processes, a secure technology infrastructure, and an efficient business model.

   Also, blockchain can increase liquidity (increases in the frequency and volume of transactions), lower capital costs (reduces commissions or operating costs), reduce counterparty risk (increases trust in transactions). It can provide opportunities for innovation in the financial industry and the development of new business models. Let's find out a little more through examples of detailed fields.

2. *Money Transfer and Settlement*

   The field that can be applied most quickly in the financial field with blockchain is in the area of money transfer and payment. If you establish a fund transfer and payment system through a blockchain, you can quickly and safely pay for goods. Above all, when trading with foreign companies, innovation can be achieved. Many import and export companies must do foreign exchange transactions for payment, but for foreign exchange transactions, they pay commissions using the services of financial institutions while taking a risk caused by exchange rate fluctuations. However, in the case of transferring funds using coins or cryptocurrency built with a blockchain, the service can be used in near real time without paying fees to the intermediary.

Libra, which was announced by Facebook in 2019, is a blockchain-based digital currency led by Facebook, and it is designed for payment or remittance using Facebook Messenger to people who do not have an account in the existing financial sector (estimated at about 1.7 billion). It is a cryptocurrency that can be used in place of currency on Facebook, with over 2.4 billion monthly users. Since it is a coin that can be exchanged at a certain rate, such as dollars and euros, once this coin is activated, we do not need to send money to friends through the bank. People can just exchange Libra on Facebook.[27] Industry experts predicted that if Facebook's Libra project, which has more than 1.5 billion daily users, succeeds, it could secure a network advantage over credit cards.

It will be a tremendous innovation if any Facebook user becomes able to send money through Facebook in real time. Facebook seems to be trying to take over a global financial network through this project. For this reason, the U.S. Congress requested that Facebook's Libra project be stopped due to risks and conflicts with the existing financial system. Behind that, the Libra project may have been a threat to the dollar, the key currency of the global financial market. Against this background, the Federal Trade Commission (FTC) approved a $5 billion fine on Facebook for several different reasons. That is why Facebook eventually announced that it would postpone the release of Libra due to concerns from the U.S. government. At present, most countries around the world recognize the dollar as the currency of the world. However, if Facebook dominates the financial network through its cryptocurrency, a tremendous shift in the financial market will occur. Therefore, many stakeholders of the current financial system seem to oppose it.

3. *Digital Identity*

Currently, to use online or offline services, in most cases, identification is required. In the past, many different types of identification

---

[27] *There is even no need for a bank account and no transaction fees.*

proof were used. Most identification proof is now performed digitally. Digital identity is information that guarantees my identity in the use of personal information on the web or various online transactions.

ID and password are the most basic identification tools, and other types of certificates are also used as digital identification tools. For example, the accredited certificate of identification widely used in South Korea contains personal information in an encrypted manner. Data points that help form a digital identity to verify your identity in various services include username and password, driver's license number, and online purchase history. The identification certificate may consist of the date of birth, online search activity, and medical records. Furthermore, for identification purposes, biometric recognition (fingerprint, iris recognition, or face recognition) patterns can also be factors that constitute an individual's identity. As data breaches rapidly increase every year, it becomes increasingly challenging to safely store and manage personally identifiable information. Incidents related to cybersecurity, such as phishing phone calls and emails and data breaches, are rising. Hackers steal information from large cyber security companies that defend against attacks with cutting-edge technologies. In addition, our personal information is collected and abused enough in various ways to look into the information stored on my smartphone. The blockchain-based digital identity management system is being proposed as a new alternative to solving this problem.

Most importantly, the current digital identity management system exhibits a low level of accessibility to many users. Many people do not have a digitized way to prove their identity. South Korea is a country where digitalization has progressed considerably. However, there is still no way to verify one's identity globally, and the credibility of the documents that can be proved is often low.[28] About 1.1 billion people around the world do not have proof of their identity. Furthermore, 45% of those who cannot prove their identity are among the poorest 20% of the planet.

Traditional identification procedures are heavily documented (e.g., various documents issued/confirmed by government offices).

---

[28] *In South Korea, ID card forgery is difficult and the background check system is well established. However, in many countries it is easy to hide one's identity with counterfeit documents.*

Therefore, cumbersome identification document processing, low accessibility (distant offices and long waiting times), and a simple lack of knowledge is a significant hurdle that puts more than 1 billion individuals in the blind spots of traditional identification systems.

Imagine that proof of identity is impossible. Without proof of identity, it is impossible to enroll in school or find a job, obtain a passport, or access many government services. People without proof of identity cannot open an account or get a loan from a bank.

On the contrary, the surprising fact is that out of the 2.7 billion people worldwide who cannot prove their identity, 60% already own a mobile phone (smartphone).[29] In such an environment, the way of identity verification is opened through a blockchain-based mobile identity solution accessible by a smartphone for people in the blind spot of an environment where identity and identity cannot be verified. If that happens, the quality of life of all these people will significantly improve.

With the development of encryption technology and the advent of blockchain technology, it has become possible to build a new ID management system, a digital identity framework based on the concept of a Decentralized Identifier (DID). Unlike existing identification methods, it is a technology in which individuals have control over their information. DID is an identity verification system made with blockchain technology. Like cryptocurrency, a distributed ledger or decentralized system replaces the user's identity verification process. The existing general identity verification system is centralized. This type of system stores the information of the people in a database established by the government and issues it upon request for proof. In other words, you can think of it as a structure that relies on the services of the central government to replace the identification of individuals. In contrast, the blockchain-based identity verification system has the characteristic that the user who is the owner of the personal information can manage and control their information.[30]

---

[29] *For some people, it seems that having a smartphone is more helpful to life than having an ID card.*

[30] *The existing system is a structure in which a specific organization instead of the individual who owns the information replaces my information and proof of identity.*

Just as we store an ID card in the wallet and take it out when necessary to prove identity, we can put the personal information in a personal blockchain wallet contained in my smartphone and enter the private key when necessary. It will change in a way that proves me.[31] Also, the high security of the blockchain technology itself and high reliability in verifying the validity of the data will allow us to use the service without worrying about the leakage of personal information and the distortion or manipulation of information during identification.

The most significant difference between an identity verification system using a blockchain and an existing authentication system is whether the validator (in the case of the government or credit information inquiry company) has personal information. The existing system is operating its own database for identity. It means that the information of the user is stored, and the user is identified through this information. However, the blockchain ID management system identifies the user by verifying it using blockchain technology. Because of that, anyone in the world can prove themselves in real time with only a smartphone. Carrying a smartphone means that you can go abroad to open an overseas bank account, get a loan, and even go to a hospital to use the service.

4. *Healthcare*

The healthcare industry is an area that can significantly benefit from blockchain technology. As everyone knows, due to aging and low fertility, most developed countries will undergo dramatic demographic changes in the near future, which is expected to lead to rapid changes and growth in the healthcare industry. For the past 30 years, the healthcare industry has maintained a centralized data system, a system that complies with past health data regulations and related laws.[32] As times change and technology advances, healthcare officials have always felt the need to digitize medical data related to the EMR (Electronic Medical Record). For this reason, it is difficult to find a place where doctors and nurses use paper charts as in the past to keep patient

---

[31] *The key factor in protecting distributed identities is encryption. In encryption, the private key is known only to the owner, and only those who hold the private key can decrypt their encrypted personal information messages.*

[32] *All patient information is kept in their own hospital and health insurance-related information is kept by government agencies.*

records. Patient information is stored using a medical information system established for each hospital and is actively used for patient management. The collected information is personal information that requires a very high level of security management. This is because the patient's hospital visit history and treatment-related information are sensitive personal information to individuals. However, it is often necessary to share among members of the medical community (hospitals, insurance companies, medical research institutions, etc.) for efficient work performance (for treatment purposes) or public purposes (for medical research and pharmaceutical development). For example, when a patient who was being treated at hospital A wants to move to hospital B to receive treatment from a doctor, how do we share the past medical records? Currently, information owned by hospitals or healthcare providers, pharmaceutical companies, and various stakeholders in the health and healthcare ecosystem is stored in a database of central systems built by each of them. It is hard to share information online or electronically in a highly efficient manner.[33]

There may be reasons due to existing laws and regulations. Still, the medical data of patients cannot be securely shared for technical reasons. Medical records are not available when a patient consults with other healthcare providers or seeks medical services or when a clinical trial manager wants to check a participant's vast medical data. Due to the incomplete management of the patient, the patient must spend valuable time and resources searching for his or her information. Due to this, redundant medical services (e.g., redundant blood tests or physical examinations) are in place, and doctors and healthcare professionals providing treatment in emergencies have limitations in real-time access to patient history (e.g., patient allergy, drug administration).

Blockchain technology enables healthcare professionals and the entire medical industry to view and utilize patients' sensitive personal data transparently and with high security in real time, thereby reducing the cost of providing efficient healthcare services and redundant services.

---

[33] *This is a method of visiting hospital A and receiving chart records as documents or submitting test and treatment records on CD to hospital B. In the 21st century, when the world is becoming digital, information sharing is taking place in this way.*

The following application can be used in the medical field using blockchain technology:

1. Safe Management of Electronic Medical Records

Blockchain enables secure, standard, and structured data sharing in the medical community (hospitals, insurance companies, pharmaceutical companies, etc.) through a distributed database. In this way, patient data and personal information are protected while sharing patient medical records only with those who need it. For this reason, information on medical service users is shared only at the required level in the medical network, and real-time inquiry is possible. Medical officials use shared data to provide efficient and high-quality medical services and reduce costs (prevent redundant examinations and treatments). Furthermore, it will promote scientific progress through effective research (because it is possible to secure an objective and accurate database).

2. Data Control by Patients

In a blockchain network environment, the right to ownership, management, and data control lies with the person who created the data. In the past, hospitals owned the data: patients had no way of controlling their hospital records. On the other hand, blockchain technology systematically can manage personal information through the privacy and authority layer of personal information (control over who can access the data: for example, doctors can see my disease history but not pharmaceutical companies). Patients cannot change or delete certain medical information entered in their profile by doctors under the blockchain framework. However, they can control all or part of their information by giving access to related institutions and personnel (e.g., a researcher belonging to a university conducting medical research).[34]

3. Improved Drug Traceability

Each hospital has its own system for the effective management of drugs. For example, in the case of drugs that are addictive or have hallucinogenic effects that should not be taken in large doses, the person

---

[34] *Currently, the individual has no way of knowing who is viewing the information and at what level the sharing takes place.*

in charge of each hospital should periodically report the type and quantity of drugs to government-related agencies. In this way, we are trying to prevent any unintended use not for administration and therapeutic purposes. However, the current management practice is that the person in charge of the hospital counts the quantity and reports the amount of prescription by hand. Under this system, the reliability of the information depends on the level of consciousness or ethics of medical personnel.[35]

By using a drug tracking system based on a blockchain, pharmaceutical companies that produce drugs can register products on the blockchain and track the movement from production to distribution to the final consumer after arriving at a medical institution. Through this process, the supervisory agency can track and manage in real time the detailed history of the drug's current location and quantity, who and for what reason it was sold, and the inventory quantity for each medical institution.

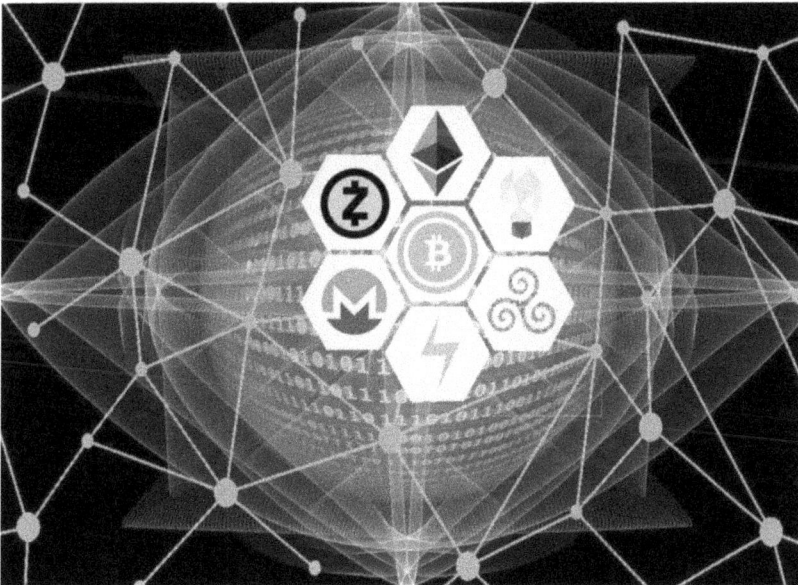

FIGURE 7.9. Block chain technology (source: "Blockchain technology" by TLC-kios is marked with CC0 1.0).

---

[35] *Therefore, sometimes drugs with high addiction are sold in hospitals through excessive or false prescriptions for the purpose of profit, and this problem emerges as a social issue.*

7.11 The Future of Blockchain

Unlike other 4th Industrial Revolution technologies, blockchain technology is the beginning stage, except for cryptocurrency, in our life and application in the industrial field.[36] This is because blockchain's potential application fields are more likely to be the fundamental changes in the current system.[37] The introduction of financial-related and digital identity verification systems using blockchains goes beyond the advantages of operation improvement, efficiency increase, cost reduction, and security improvement. It is expected that blockchain will make improvements and innovations in how the economic/business system operates.

Even though its merits are evident, there may be a limit to disseminating related technologies within a short period due to conflicts of interest among stakeholders.[38] It will fundamentally replace the existing process beyond the level of merely creating value through technology. However, the potential of blockchain is endless. It will be a technology that will be more noteworthy because we believe that it will create new jobs and expand business opportunities while dramatically improving our lives.

---

[36] *There are various ideas and business applications using blockchain, but other than cryptocurrency, the level we experience is at a low level.*

[37] *As described previously, the motivation behind the creation of the blockchain was to solve the problems of the existing financial system, and there are many application fields for improvement and replacement of systems that make up and move society, such as digital identity verification/health information system/smart contracts, etc.*

[38] *Existing financial sectors and governments that fear Facebook's cryptocurrency "Libra" are good examples. There will be fierce resistance from existing interest groups such as brokers, which will disappear due to smart contract technology, and the stakeholders who have been profiting from the existing social system.*

CHAPTER 8

ROBOTICS AND AUTOMATION

8.1 Robotics and Automation

Many general users used the "repeat click" macro to apply for a desired class when enrolling in a college and reserve concert tickets for famous singers. Some have called it a keyboard mouse macro recording program. In the past, automation was at the level of recording repetitive tasks using a keyboard and mouse. However, now we can add the requirements we think of and automatically select and execute complex functions according to those conditions, and we call them robotics and automation. Let us take a closer look at robotics and automation.

8.2 Introduction to Robotics and Automation

Robotics and automation are fields that develop rapidly in combination with artificial intelligence, and they automate simple and repetitive tasks and perform them quickly and precisely. Thanks to these advantages, they are widely used in corporate finance, accounting, manufacturing, purchasing, and customer management. However, automation using the current robotics can only handle tasks with clearly defined rules and is not at a level that completely replaces human judgment. If technologies such as artificial intelligence and machine learning are applied to robotics and automation, it will be possible to replace even high-level tasks that only humans can do. Applying cognitive technologies such as machine learning, speech recognition, and natural language processing can be used for cancer diagnosis in medical fields that require human cognitive ability, customer asset management in the financial industry, and legal precedents analysis.

If automation using robotics is implemented, the daily work within the organization can also be reduced. For example, it is estimated that more than half of the current business operations can apply to robotics and automation. Much of what we do is spending a lot of time and energy on simple repetitive tasks. These repetitive tasks are an area that can be applied to robotics and automation. One Asian commercial bank implemented automation by introducing robotics and automation for 183 operations. It is expected that a total of 1.25 million hours will be reduced in terms of working hours. Assuming an average of 2,000 hours worked per employee per year, this means that simple repetitive tasks involving more than 600 people were automated through robots.[1]

Table 8.1. Example of Cost Reduction Effect When Robot Automation Is Introduced

Type	Cost	Availability
Traditional Onshore Labor	$120,000 / year	40 hours per week
Offshore Labor	$50,000 / year	40 hours per week
Software Robot (Digital Labor)	$15,000 / year	24 hours / 7 days

8.3 What Is a Robot in Robotics and Automation?

Robots are mechanical devices that can automatically perform specific tasks or operations. The robot may be controlled by an external control device or may have a built-in control device. Although the robot may represent a human shape, it may be designed as a robot with an inhuman form considering only the characteristics and purpose of the work. For example, while humanoid robots appear a lot in movies, various robots are made for particular purposes in factories, such as robot arms specialized only for welding.

---

[1] *https://www.uipath.com/resources/automation-case-studies/kb-kookmin-bank-banking-rpa*

FIGURE 8.1 Robot arm (source: "File:KUKA Industrial Robot Writer.jpg" by Mirko Tobias Schäfer is licensed under CC BY 2.0).

Robots can replace many tasks in the industrial field. Robots can replace monotonous, repetitive, tedious, and dangerous jobs that exist in industrial sites. Examples include riveting, welding, and painting of automobile bodies in assembly plants. Robots do not require frequent breaks like humans and can produce products of consistent quality. They can be actively used for the process of mass production.

Robots can take over dangerous tasks that humans cannot do or work in extreme situations. For example, when handling radioactive materials or toxic chemicals, robots can work without wearing protective clothing. In addition, robots can work in harsh environments with temperatures that are too high or too low to allow humans to perform. Robots can be used in environments that can threaten human life, such as searching for explosives, detonating bombs, or working in outer space.

Most of the robots we think of and imagine are in the physical form described previously. However, in addition to the physical robots that we generally think of, other types of robots already exist in our lives and help a lot. Let us take a look at software robots now.

8.4 Software Robot?

A macro refers to a system that combines several frequently used commands into a single keystroke operation. These macros are widely used in that they can learn repetitive tasks of computers or humans. For example, macros were mainly used for automatic battle and hunting in computer games. Even if the user does not specify a target individually, it kills prey and collects resources. Due to this convenience, it has been a necessity for heavy gamers in the online game era.

These macros can also be used when doing a lot of work in a company. As macros replace repetitive and tedious tasks, humans can focus on more creative and higher-level jobs. Automation using robotics is a software-type automation robot that realizes this desire. Robotics and automation in the simple form are similar to a "macro," a program that repeats simple movements. But there is a lot more you can do.

For example, suppose an employee checks customer information daily, organizes it in Excel, and prints it on paper. If this is less than 10 cases per day, it will be fine, but as the number of cases becomes 100 or 1,000, more time and economic resources are being invested, which can be inefficient compared to investment. What if the robot handles this at a set time every morning according to a set scenario? Whether there are 100 or 10,000 documents, there is no need to worry. It is because, as you know, robots are not tired 24 hours a day, work quality is uniform, and processing speeds are much faster than humans.

Therefore, software robots' introduction is more effective in companies with larger workplaces and frequent document processing tasks. Nowadays, when working from home has become more common due to COVID-19, the number of companies considering automation through robots for more efficient workforce management and work improvement is increasing significantly. Let's take a closer look at the meaning of automation.

8.5 What Is Automation in Robotics and Automation?

Automation, in simple terms, means that work is done automatically through a computer or programmed software. Automation or computerization in modern society has significant meaning because mechanical power was introduced into existing production activities that depended on labor power to automate processes.

There are three main types of automation:

- Office automation
- Factory automation
- Home automation

8.5.1 Office Automation

In the case of office automation, it is an automation system developed to handle a company's office work. For example, balance and interest calculations on bank customer accounts can be automated with data processing systems. The devices used include computers, word processors, facsimile machines, and copiers.

8.5.2 Factory Automation

Factory automation automates the life and death process of a factory and mainly uses computers and various measuring equipment. It can range from automating the production process of making a product to automating the entire process of ordering and shipping products to customers in a narrow range.

8.5.3 Home Automation

Home automation refers to a system that allows you to automatically control all home appliances, heating appliances, windows, and even the entrance door from outside the house through a phone or smartphone. Through this remote-control function, devices in the house can be used effectively, and accidents such as gas leakage, fire, and theft can be responded to quickly and effectively.

8.6 The Evolution of Software Robots

In modern society, software robots have translated human cognitive functions beyond replacing simple repetitive tasks by fusion with technologies like artificial intelligence and machine learning. Let us take a look at how these software robots have evolved gradually.

Early forms of robots had their main task in doing what they were commanded to do. In other words, the main expected area was to perform repetitive tasks precisely as directed by the user. It was a good fit for rules-based processes where compliance and accuracy were substantial.

These software robots face new changes as they encounter artificial intelligence and machine learning. If the existing robots were at the level of performing as commanded, the robots could now learn themselves. In other words, even if the process is not accurately defined and structured, learning and decision-making are made based on a large amount of data. There is a great advantage in improving abilities while continuously performing tasks through the function of self-learning. Therefore, considering the improvement of productivity and quality over a long period, introducing an artificial intelligence robot capable of self-learning and evolution can be considered an effective method.

However, at the current level of technology, it can be said that automating existing simple tasks or standardized work processes is a more stable technology than artificial intelligence automation. For this reason, there are still more automation cases that do not use artificial intelligence.

8.7 Automation Example Using Robotics

Then, let us look at an example of automation using robots. Let us take a real company job as an example. Suppose you have an employee at a company, and one of his jobs is to reflect the system of emails from essential customers immediately. In this case, if robot automation is applied, the following commands can be designed:

1. Log in to the corporate mail system

2. Read when a specific sender's mail arrives

3. Download attached file when specific word or form comes

4. Text excerpt in the specified location of the attached file

5. Company system login

6. Enter and save the extracted text in the company system

7. Send SMS or email to the person in charge in case of unexpected error

8. Write completion record after completion of work

The design and construction of such robotic automation start from imitating human behavior and, in other words, designing and imitating existing human behavior patterns as data. If this automation is fused with artificial intelligence, the dependence of data on human behavior and overall processes may increase. The procedure for performing robot automation, designed as an example, was intended as a straightforward process. Still, in reality, it can be effectively applied to more complex and lengthy general tasks.

8.8 Robotics Misunderstandings and Truth

According to what we have learned so far, many tasks that humans have done can be replaced through robotics. Robots are replacing many jobs, and more complex tasks will also be possible. Robots are inexpensive, sustainable and, unlike humans, they do not tire or make errors from a business standpoint. As a result, people anticipate many jobs to disappear in the future. Therefore, due to these concerns, there is a negative perspective on automation using many robots. Let's take a look at the misconceptions and truths of robotics.

Misconception: Robots can solve problems by themselves.

Reality: Robots need some human help to solve problems.

Robots cannot solve existing processes or problems themselves. The robot can get rid of repetitive work in doing your job, but it is a misunderstanding that the robot will solve the problem itself.

Misconception: Robots can improve all processes.

Reality: Automation using robots is a technology that connects existing broken systems and processes.

There are tens of thousands of processes simultaneously in business processes (sales/personnel/IT/financial/accounting, etc.). These processes include sequential and quantitative/qualitative methods that require human judgment in charge. For example, when a recruitment task is performed among the personnel work process, it is possible to automate the recruitment announcement, résumé screening, and onboarding process through a robot. However, a process such as an interview is not easy to automate. That is still a unique area for humans.

Misconception: Robots will replace humans.

Reality: Humans will focus on their domains that only humans can do: results, analysis, and relationships.

Robots will, to some extent, replace human jobs and change the types and futures of jobs. Along with technological development, this has occurred to some extent. For example, process or task that had been done manually were replaced by computers. Currently, many call center personnel are being replaced by chatbots. The social change in the organizational structure and necessary workforce caused by technology is natural. Humans can now focus on high-level analysis/consulting/creative tasks rather than simple functions with robots' evolution. For example, data collection is replaced by the IoT, and humans perform tasks of analyzing collected data, interpreting meaning, and applying.

8.9 Automation Application Area Using Robots

In this section, let us look at the fields where automation using robots is possible.

8.9.1 Invoice Processing

Documents that indicate the main details of the transaction are called invoices. These invoices refer to the statement of goods traded by the sender to the consignee and serve as an invoice to the exporter. The more invoices your company processes, the more repetitive manual work you have. It can result in delays or errors in payment. According to a study by technology services firm Aberdeen Group, it takes between 4.1 and 16.3 days for companies to process an invoice after issuing a receipt and receiving approval for payment. It is not just a matter of time but because employees have to process each invoice if they do it manually. In fact, according to the Cannon Business Process Services survey, more than half of invoice processing requires at least 76–100% manual entry.[2]

These numbers clearly show that companies are unfortunately missing out on that possibility despite increasing their finance and accounting departments' efficiency sufficiently in this era of increasing digitization and automation. The high proportion of manual work is relatively inefficient due to the lack of centralized management or standardized invoice management. Also, it does not stop at inefficiencies. It means that there is a possibility that the company might fail to manage its invoices, resulting in arrears

---

[2] *https://www.uipath.com/blog/uipath-at-work-automating-the-invoice-process*

due to unpaid invoices, unnecessary labor costs, or even higher costs. When incoming invoices arrive in their respective formats, such as paper copies, Word documents, PDF email attachments, or faxes, the company's finance team needs to convert the data in these various invoice formats into their database. In the case of data inconsistency in manual transmission, this must also be handled with responsibility. Software robots can automate some of the decisions that finance managers require when processing invoices, such as data entry and error reconciliation. Simultaneously, you can limit errors in these processes and reduce the number of exceptions that require manual handling.

8.9.2 Sales and Customer Service

Many companies currently use the ERP system to take advantage of business processes such as ordering, billing, and deposit. However, there are still many manual tasks, such as entering new vendors, registration, sales data verification, settlement, data verification (communication), and so on. In addition, customer complaints are received in the field of customer service, detailed complaint data is entered, and the person in charge is contacted. Many tasks include identifying and solving problems, getting customers for periodic status updates, continuously tracking and checking problem cases, and closing cases when solving issues are carried out by hand. It is possible to rescue efficient processes for tracking management, manual data input, and communication between departments after receiving customer complaints through robot automation.

8.9.3 Data Science Field

Uncleaned data is called messy data, and cleaning messy data is called cleaning or scrubbing. If the ratio of messy data among the information is above a certain level, statistics and analysis results become meaningless. Therefore, it is necessary to clean up messy data in preparation for data analysis. Suppose you need to perform data analysis to evaluate your company's sales performance. There is raw data collected now, but this data is not all meaningful and necessary data. A lot of information is often meaningless or worthless. Purifying such messy data and performing data cleaning occupies a large part in the actual data analysis work. Robot automation can be effectively substituted for data cleaning tasks that consume a lot of time and energy.

8.9.4 Compliance

The area of compliance in corporate management is gradually expanding. It is because compliance is slowly growing from legal adherence to corporate norms and social norms. Compliance was initially started in the financial field, but today it expands to various areas such as fair trade, corruption prevention, and environmental issues. Many countries also have compliance laws. Compliance issues can lead to ethical problems, reputational risks, and financial losses such as legal penalties or fines. Many of these compliance tasks are now dependent on manual work. It is necessary to periodically check and approve whether the existing process is complied with or for related documents, but this part is expected to be replaced by robot automation.

8.9.5 Marketing

Robots can be actively used for automated marketing campaigns. Many of the existing marketing tasks rely on manual techniques. For example, to collect customer data, methods such as surveys or customer interviews are used. The customer information is collected and surveyed by phone or survey while spending a lot of money. If you use a robot to automate this, you can get high cost-effectiveness. For example, nowadays, data is collected from social media and online blogs to identify customer preferences and trends. It is possible to check customer reactions by automatically collecting and analyzing necessary information online through web scraping. This series of marketing tasks can be automated using robots.

In addition to this, automation is possible in the following business areas:

8.9.6 Finance

- Processing of approval and rejection of non-face-to-face account opening
- The identification of identity card authenticity
- Credit rating inquiry and Excel report creation from external sites
- Collecting investment analysis information

8.9.7 Manufacturing

- Inquiry of bill of materials data for material and production management

- Automation of ERP input
- Product price and work cost billing process automation
- Inventory and net shipment amount verification

8.9.8 Distribution

- Inventory management input and approval process
- Point of sale data input, work, the reporting process
- Product import/export shipping document processing automation
- Monthly closing work processing automation
- Corporate card, travel expenses, purchase tax invoice processing automation

8.9.9 IT Tasks

- Manual tasks related to maintenance, data cleaning tasks
- IT support tasks (case opening, tracking management, future maintenance, etc.)

FIGURE 8.2. Examples of the automation application area using robots.

8.10 Areas That Are Difficult to Apply

Although the robot's applicability is diverse, there are also limitations depending on the work's characteristics. Let us see what areas are difficult to automate using robots.

8.10.1 Customer Service

Although it is possible to provide customer service such as simple customer counseling and question answering through chatbots, emotional communication and communication with real customers can be said to be a field that humans must perform directly. Many companies use robots to support customer service, but it is unlikely that this change can replace all existing human service customer services. Communicating with customers and exchanging emotions would be difficult to expect from a robot of the current level.

8.10.2 Sales and Marketing

Simple repetitive tasks required for sales activities can be automated through robots, but establishing customer relationships, which are essential parts of sales, and in-depth communication with customers are areas that robots cannot perform at this time. Marketing activities that require creative thinking, such as planning the creative promotion of products, and building and setting brand images, are also areas that only humans, not robots, can be in charge of.

8.10.3 Human Resource Management

Among the existing human resource work processes, repetitive and mechanical work can be automated through robots. However, the areas that require close relationships and thinking between humans, such as workforce education, leadership development, face-to-face interviews, and teamwork establishment, are areas that robots cannot perform.

In addition to the previously introduced areas, in areas where human creativity, empathy, and cognitive ability are mainly required, it is not easy to expect complete automation of robots with the current technology level. In the future, if the remarkable growth of artificial intelligence creates human-like intellectual abilities and emotions, these areas may also be automated by robots.

8.11 Benefits through Robotic Process Automation

The most significant advantage of introducing robotic automation is its high Return on Investment (ROI). Early robotic automation aimed to replace tasks that were simple, repetitive, and inefficient for humans to do. The current robotic automation is expanding beyond this to automating system infrastructure and processes within an organization. Automation through robots has a higher ROI than building IT systems, including ERP. Implementation difficulty is also low, and user satisfaction is increased after the introduction. The advantages and effects of automation using robots are as follows:

8.11.1 Accuracy

Data errors are prevented, and data integrity is guaranteed through input automation. It reduces the need and effort of rework to correct the mistakes.

8.11.2 Efficiency

Robot automation can further focus the existing workforce on high value-added activities. For example, simple repetitive tasks rely on robots, and humans can put more effort into continuous work improvement.

8.11.3 Quickness

Robots can work 24/7. In simple, repetitive, mechanical precision, or dangerous tasks for humans, high risk can be performed through robot automation. Through the robot's control device, the scale of work can be quickly and gradually adjusted.

8.11.4 Improve Employee Satisfaction

Robots replace tedious, repetitive, or dangerous tasks for humans to improve workers' satisfaction and quality of life. By entrusting more value-added tasks to employees, employees' morale, loyalty, and motivation to work can be improved.

8.11.5 Accelerate Productivity Improvement

A single robot can replace the tasks of several humans. Since robots do not require shifts or many breaks like humans, they can significantly contribute to accelerating the process's productivity. More efficient human resources management becomes possible. By replacing simple, repetitive, high-risk tasks with robots, it is possible to reduce the incidence and cost of human accidents. Improving productivity by robotic automation can bring greater profits to organizations.

8.11.6 Enhance Compliance

Since the robot automatically executes only humans' commands, compliance with the regulations of the process can be strengthened. This consistent and clear compliance process can make it easier to audit and trace any errors or problems in the process.

8.12 Actual Application Examples

Finally, let us look at the actual business application cases using robotics and automation.

8.12.1 Medical Field

In Dublin, Ireland, the Mater Misericordiae University Hospital uses robots from robotic automation platform company UiPath to process COVID-19 screening kits. It reduces the administrative burden imposed on the infection prevention management department by receiving patient test results in real time. With all nurses accessing the robot, the hospital's medical staff saves about three hours a day and devotes their spare time to caring for patients. COVID-19 has changed the working environment of hospitals. Hospitals that have to deal with numerous documents have added diseases to be managed quickly and continuously, and severe infections have maximized the demand for data processing. It is because the workload other than data processing has also increased. Robotic automation is helping the medical staff to focus on other tasks while separating them from data tasks.

Daniel Dines, CEO of UiPath, said, "We are receiving a lot of investment to cope with the spread of COVID-19 with the help of robotic automation platforms and to provide support for our customers as they transition to a new operating model." That's why he argues that robotic automation can change the healthcare industry. The aftermath of COVID-19 has accelerated the need for system change. Accordingly, robot automation software is provided free of charge to medical institutions, and as practical results have appeared, attempts to introduce robot automation into the medical industry are exploding.

8.12.2 Article Writing

The Associated Press (AP), a media company based in New York City, is a good example. AP has started providing automated corporate performance reports to other media since 2014. The AP struggled to find a way to increase the volume of articles and enhance the company's brand image without incurring additional costs. Lou Ferrara, AP's vice president and editor-in-chief, led the service automation business. He found that journalists prefer to report on articles that require creativity and that through such creative work, they show their value the most. Most reporters hated highly structured jobs such as reporting on corporate performance. By automating corporate reports, AP was able to increase the volume of articles at no cost. The number of corporate reports prepared by AP was about 300 per quarter when previously written by humans but grew to more than 3,700 after using software robots.

Along with the advantage of creating more content, automation has saved the time equivalent to the workload of three full-time reporters. The AP's unionized reporters were able to keep their jobs, and customers were satisfied with the articles' quality and fast reporting. After introducing the automation company report, AP has also pursued a similar automation project to expand college sports articles.

8.12.3 Customer Service

The "Erica" service, a self-managed virtual assistant of the Bank of America (BOA), could be an example. Erica is an artificial intelligence robot that analyzes its customers' account balances to warn of over-consumption and provides personalized services such as recommending favorable card payment dates for customers.

In addition, Mizuho Bank has deployed SoftBank's emotion recognition robot "Pepper" in bank stores nationwide that responds to customers. Through Pepper, customers can search for financial information provided by Mizuho Bank. Also, Pepper is being used as a universal concierge by applying artificial intelligence technology already used in call centers.

Another large U.S. bank redesigned its customer complaints process, developed 85 software robots, and automatically operated 13 operations to automatically handle 1.5 million complaints per year. As a result, the bank secured an additional processing capacity equivalent to 230 full-time employees and reduced costs by about 30% compared to hiring more employees. Also, the percentage of completing tasks "in just one shot" increased by 27%. In this way, companies can use robots to execute new processes that were unrealistic in the past, beyond automation of existing processes, and thus can see cost savings.[3]

8.12.4 Distribution Field

ShopDirect, a UK distribution company, applies robot process automation to identify customers whose payments are delayed due to flooding and automatically handle late fees, thereby automating the work that many workers had done manually.

8.12.5 Extract Data

It is time-consuming and expensive for humans to collect data from various sources. Software robots can use intelligent optical character recognition and natural language processing capabilities to research distributed information from various sources. The robot extracts critical data from multiple sources and then transmits the collected information to its database. Then, the robot can process related tasks through relevant information. The form of the data source and the data condition that can be extracted can appear in various formats such as editable text, handwritten memos, online web page data, and APIs. With robots, the entire process can be automated with little to no compromise on the information's accuracy. You will be able to save time and energy for many employees and focus on more productive tasks.

8.12.6 Processing Human Resource Information

When it comes to personnel work, you will first think of payroll management, employee recruitment, retirement, and promotion. The company's information changes from time to time and needs to be maintained over time, but these tasks are not always new or creative. The scope of management is vast, and there are many repetitive manual tasks. Robots can help when you have to work mechanically for an extended period due to a small amount of work. The introduction of robotic automation effectively reduces these monotonous manual tasks. For this reason, many companies and human resource service providers are using robotic process automation to digitize data-driven processes to improve work efficiency. Also, automation of the hiring process can significantly streamline the overall hiring process. Recruitment robots

---

[3] *David Schatsky, Craig Muraskin, and Kaushik Iyengar. 2017. Robotic process automation, A path to the cognitive enterprise. New York: Deloitte Consulting.*

can be responsible for sourcing resumes on different platforms, reviewing résumés, and screening people to invite to in-person interviews.

8.13 The Future of Robot Automation

In modern society, robotic automation can streamline corporate processes, improve productivity, and improve employee and customer satisfaction. At the current technology level, robotic automation processes that replace simple repetitive tasks are mainly supplied to industries. With the remarkable growth of artificial intelligence, it is expected that robot automation will further expand in the near future. Beyond the execution of simple and repetitive tasks, it will be possible to perform decisions that only humans could have made, and to have emotional exchanges with humans, self-learning, and self-development. If robot automation with intelligence comparable to humans is built like this, a day may arrive when robots can automatically oversee all company processes.

INDEX

business applications of
  digital identity, 103–106
  financial sector, 102
  healthcare industry, 106–107
  in medical field, 108–109
  money transfer and settlement,
    102–103
defined, 95
distributed ledger technology, 89n9
future of, 110
origin of, 91–93
types of
  hybrid, 101
  private, 100–101
  public, 100–101
working pattern of, 95–96
Business analytics, 10–11

C

Central Bank, 86
Chatbot, 47
Cloud computing. *See also* Big data
    analytics; Internet of Things
    (IoT)
  advantages of, 27–28
    agriculture, 34
    entertainment, 34
    healthcare, 33
  defined, 22–23
  infrastructure as a service (IaaS)
    method (*see* Infrastructure as a
    service (IaaS) method)
  platform as a service (PaaS) method
    (*see* Platform as a service (PaaS)
    method)
  service providers, 36
  software as a service (SaaS) method
    (*see* Software as a Service (SaaS)
    method)
Cloud services model, 27
  hybrid cloud, 33

  private cloud, 32–33
  public cloud, 31–33
COVID-19, 20, 114
CPU, 22
Cross-border money transaction, 98–99
CrowdStrike, 36
Cryptocurrency, 85, 95
  process of exchange of, 97
Cybersecurity, 36

D

Data. *See also* Big data
  generation speed, 39
  structured, 38
  unstructured, 38
  veracity, 39
Data analytics, 10–11
Data storage, 19
Datawarehouse, 36, 36n9
Decentralized identifier (DID), 105
Deep learning, 56–61. *See also* Artificial
    intelligence; Machine learning
Depository Trust & Clearing Corporation
    (DTCC), 87
Double-spending problem, 94–95

E

Economic transactions, 86
Enterprise resource planning (ERP)
    system, 23, 28
Ethereum, 100

F

Fedwire (formerly known as Federal
    Reserve Wire Network), 86
Financial firms, 87
Financial institutions, 86
Financial markets, 86
Financial products, 86

www.ingramcontent.com/pod-product-compliance
Lightning Source LLC
Chambersburg PA
CBHW081540220326
41598CB00036B/6503

9 781683 926887